"It's a timeless test - of patience."

You can become a Shareholder of Lord's Plc

- *Lord's Ground Match Seat for Life*

- *No more queuing*

- *Shareholding in Lord's Plc*

- *Share transferable for value*

- *Dividend income*

- *Introduction of Company Law*

- *Termination of arbitrary committee government*

- *A world class Body Corporate – the MCC*

* Go to www.mccsgm.org.uk to bring about change at Lord's *

Password – Ward2025

You can become a Shareholder of Lord's Plc

- *Lord's Ground Match Seat for Life*

- *No more queuing*

- *Shareholding in Lord's Plc*

- *Share transferable for value*

- *Dividend income*

- *Introduction of Company Law*

- *Termination of arbitrary committee government*

- *A world class Body Corporate – the MCC*

* Go to <u>www.mccsgm.org.uk</u>
to bring about change at Lord's *

Password – Ward2025

TUNNEL VISION AT LORD'S

WITH A FOREWORD BY
SIR CLIVE LLOYD

BY
NIGEL KNOTT

Knott Publishing

© Copyright 2025 Nigel Knott

All rights reserved. No part of this publication may be reproduced, stored in a retrieval system, or transmitted, in any form or by any means, electronic, mechanical, photocopying, recording, or otherwise, without the written prior permission of the author.

The Moral Right of the author has been asserted.

First Published in 2025 by Nigel Knott.

Hard cover Print Edition:
ISBN 978-1-0683976-0-8

Soft cover Print Edition:
978-1-0683976-2-2

Electronic Book Edition:
978-1-0683976-1-5

A CIP catalogue record for this book is available from the British Library.

Knott Publishing
Knap Cottage, Seend SN12 6NN. UK.

Dedication

To Rosemary, my beloved wife for sixty years, for her patience and tolerance in support of my mission to preserve Lord's as the greatest ground in the world for playing international cricket matches. Also, to Keith Bradshaw and John Reason – may they rest in peace.

Contents

Foreword by Sir Clive Lloyd 1

Introduction 5

Chapter 1 A Warrior Family 29

Chapter 2 A Club in Conflict 45

Chapter 3 The Wrong People in the Wrong Jobs 65

Chapter 4 Meetings and Machinations 81

Chapter 5 The ECB – A Cuckoo in the Lord's Nest 93

Chapter 6 Tunnels and a Train Crash 111

Chapter 7 What Is the Point of MCC? 127

Chapter 8 Trustees and a Lack of Trust 149

Chapter 9 Chairmen and Conundrums 161

Chapter 10 A Vision Failure 179

Chapter 11 A New Landlord at Lord's
Documenting the changes needed 199

Chapter 12 Conclusion 207

Postscript 223

Index 227

"You can tell it's dawn when you hear the MCC members' chorus of disapproval about queuing for seats."

Foreword by Sir Clive Lloyd

It is very heartening to read that Dr Knott's views and mine coincide as regards the commercialisation of international cricket and the proposal to rank Test-playing nations. Only recently, I spoke against the latter development. Dr Knott calls it a manufactured change to the traditions of the game which could have a negative effect on the game in West Indies. For this he must be commended. He must be commended, too, for his efforts in seeking to make his club, MCC, a self-governing body owned by its shareholders. In the final analysis this publication is a good addition to the wonderful literature on cricket and the many problems it has faced during the course of its evolution.

Dr Knott, as he says, is a long-standing member of MCC. I was intrigued therefore by his narration of the historical background of his club and the role it has played in the expansion of cricket globally. I say intrigued because any West Indian would know that after the founding of the club in 1787 and its purchase in 1866, it went on to be one of the major purveyors of the game overseas. MCC and other English teams visited the Caribbean as early as 1896/1897. This first team was led by A A Priestley. MCC first toured the Caribbean also in 1910/1911. And since these first contacts between the Caribbean and MCC (the last England tour under its banner was in 1973-74) all manner of English teams have been coming to our shores. It is interesting to note that during this early period West Indian cricket was in its embryonic stage. There is no doubt that our cricket learnt and benefited from these tours. The role of MCC and England in the development of West Indian cricket, to which Dr Knott referred, is acknowledged.

Also, it was the interaction of the cricketing authorities from both sides that led to the involvement of West Indian players in the leagues and county cricket. This led to West Indian players' outstanding contribution to English cricket. As Dr Knott has noted, English cricket could not help but benefit from the presence of Weekes, Walcott, Kanhai, Sobers, Hall, Ramadhin, Valentine and Roy Marshall, among many others. I am happy that I made a modest contribution, turning out in my colours for Lancashire. Dr Knott is correct: West Indian players played for the benefit of all concerned.

It is a good point, inferred by him, that cricket was not touched at this time by the deadening hand of the commercialisation of the game. Cricketers, as I can attest, played for the love of the game. Now Moloch has entered the ranks. I must agree with Dr Knott that the commercialisation of international cricket has had a deleterious effect on international cricket generally and specifically on Caribbean cricket. This is already evident. We cannot field the best Test team. Our best players have been seduced by lucrative contracts associated with franchise cricket.

Dr Knott is quite right. We have been a loyal member of the ICC for more than 100 years and we have been a cash cow for many by drawing large crowds at all of the main venues in the world. Now that we are in a period of rebuilding, we need the understanding and a return on our playing the most attractive cricket in the world and drawing, as a consequence, sold-out crowds. I regard it as a vote of confidence that Dr Knott also believes that the far flung West Indian islands need extra resources which we will not get if we are confined to playing weaker teams. Here the question of ranking teams and the commercialisation of the game intersect. I believe that the decision to rank international Test-playing teams is a ploy to attract greater resources for the so-called better teams. I referred to the positive impact the touring MCC and English cricket teams had on the development of our cricket. The point cannot be lost that weaker teams can only improve if they play stronger teams. India, Pakistan and Sri Lanka were once regarded as the minnows of Test cricket. Now they challenge and conquer the best. I hope the administrators of the game study its evolution carefully and come to the right decision. Here too Dr Knott is in the vanguard. It is for the players of the game to set the standards, not the less discerning bureaucrats. The attempt to monetise this noble game with players becoming mercenaries is not the answer to the problems of modern cricket.

Every cricketer wants to play at Lord's. No one would contest Dr Knott's claim that it is one of the meccas of cricket. At Lord's, West Indian cricket has on occasion risen to great heights, as in 1950 when we defeated England for the first time. This victory allowed our fans free reign to express themselves in song and dance. The sense of history was palpable also in 1963 when the Test match came to a dramatic conclusion. The case for Lord's remaining a hallowed venue is unarguable.

I therefore support the efforts of Dr Knott to ensure that the traditions are maintained and that MCC must be an independent entity as it plays a role in helping the administrators to overcome the difficulties cricket is now facing. Lord's should have more, not less cricket, and all of the great Test-playing nations must be able to display their genius for the game in various ways there, for it is one of the truly beautiful cricket grounds. If I understand Dr. Knott correctly, the threat to Lord's as a venue for more, not less, cricket is connected with the proposal to rank Test teams. He clearly implies that the ECB will go along with this suggestion. I therefore support Dr Knott in his campaign to ensure that the traditional structure of the game is maintained and Lord's remains a trusted venue of international competition of the highest standard.

LORD'S IN DANGER.
THE M. C. C. GO OUT TO MEET THE ENEMY.
[" Sir EDWARD WATKIN *proposes to construct a Railway passing through Lord's Cricket Ground.*"]

Members of MCC have no democratic or effective say in Club governance, they may as well be members of an 18th century private members club. Your membership ceases when you die!

You can instead be a Shareholder of a Royal Charter Corporation with at least £1.5 billion in assets, with a legacy to pass on to your heirs!

To sign up as a Shareholder visit
www.mccsgm.org.uk
and enter the Password – *Ward2025*

Introduction

Our precious heritage endowed for the guardianship of Marylebone Cricket Club members is forgotten all too easily.

Lord's, without the benevolent action of William Ward in 1824, would today be part of an upmarket residential estate in north London. It is a complete mystery on what terms Thomas Lord held the present ground when he took possession in June 1813; as is the case with the granting of a formal long lease to Ward in 1835 by the Eyre family. On learning of Lord's proposal to build four semi-detached houses along St John's Wood Road boundary and another three along the Eyre estate boundary – the building of St John's Wood Church in 1814 had prompted the construction of many residential properties across the road from the ground – Ward bought his interest for £5,400 on 1st January 2024 (Eyre Estate records).

His first act was to enlarge and decorate the wooden pavilion, erected in 1814, which he did at great expense. In the early hours of July 29 1825, the day following the Harrow v Winchester College match, the entire building was consumed by fire. Firemen attended the blaze from all over London but by 5 a.m. there remained only the burnt-out embers of the pavilion, the club records and its valuable wine cellar. Ward performed the remarkable feat of completing the new replacement pavilion in time for the anniversary dinner on May 11 1826.

Ward, who was born in 1787, the year of the founding of MCC, was educated at Winchester College and became one of the best-known financiers of his generation. In 1817 he was a director of the Bank of England and in 1826 he became a Tory MP for the City of London. In 1835, a year after the formation of the Conservative Party led by Sir Robert Peel, he lost his parliamentary seat to the Whigs and departed from public life. His talents as a leading batsman had also become apparent in his early days. His cricketing feats included a record-breaking 278 playing for MCC at Lord's in 1820 against a Norfolk X1. This mammoth innings began on his 33rd birthday when he occupied the crease spread over a three-day period. This record was broken in 1925 by Percy Holmes, (an unbeaten 315) and one year after that by Jack Hobbs (an unbeaten 316).

On June 30 1835 Walpole Eyre granted Ward a 59-year lease and on July 4 that same year James Dark bought Ward's interest in return for £2,000 and an annuity payable to the Ward family until the lease expired. Dark became the caretaker of Lord's and made many significant improvements during his tenure. MCC owes much to his hard work and dedication to developing and maintaining it into a cricket ground with an enviable reputation. However, with his health failing, he decided to transfer his interest to MCC in 1864. He had earlier urged the club to buy the ground at auction from the Eyre estate when the committee failed to make a bid and the Lord's freehold passed into the ownership of Isaac Moses for £7,000.

Dark had been the proprietor for nearly 30 years and refused many tempting offers for housing development. He remained steadfast in his wish to transfer his interest to MCC. The names of both Ward and Dark should remain in the affections of cricketers the world over and particularly in those of MCC members in perpetuity.

On March 26 1866 William Nicholson rode to MCC's rescue to provide the mortgage money necessary to purchase Lord's for £18,333 6s 8d. Completion took place on August 22 that year. Nicholson was another well-known figure in London with his gin bottles sporting what became the MCC 'egg and bacon' colours. To these MCC titans, the name of Lord (Charles) Russell must be remembered for his 67 years of loyal MCC membership. He was a purist extolling the virtues of the English national game played at the home of the professors of the traditional values of cricket who rejected the increasingly popular sport of 'swiping and hurling.' Plus ça change! The time is long overdue for MCC to recognise the achievements of these generous legators with a fitting tribute. Not that this has been suggested. When attempting in 2022 (unsuccessfully) to drop the Eton v Harrow fixture, dating back to 1805, the committee conveniently overlooked how much they owed to an Old Harrovian (Nicholson).

The ECB bean counters are determining the future. They seem to have forgotten the players themselves who are fast becoming mercenaries. Never has the game become so polarised with so many different formats and so much player confusion. The cliché 'it's not cricket' has never rung so true. The Hundred seems to be here to stay as a professional sport and how the laws of cricket can be manipulated so dramatically defeats me. It will not be long before the sacred design of the cricket bat and cricket ball will become unrecognisable.

To those of us who experienced the days of the amateur and the professional cricketer, it comes as no surprise to witness the monetisation of the game itself. Indeed, the very definition of 'cricket' now requires a much clearer definition as the game is being secularised with a clash of cultures within the very woolsack of cricket itself at Lord's.

The mouth-watering sum of nearly £150m paid by a Silicon Valley tech consortium in January 2025 for a franchise team playing in The Hundred at Lord's does not even mean that they own a piece of the turf. Many years ago, a member of MCC's committee, Lord Derby, believed the club should emulate the success of the Jockey Club and today an 11-strong syndicate has bought a racehorse in the name of 'London Spirit.' The new owners must hope they can win the equivalent of the London Derby to justify their investment.

The breathtaking market valuations confirm what was known

already: that Lord's is the winner by a distance. One can only hope the rather sleepy MCC members will awake from their reverie and stare reality in the face. It is well known that the 17.5 acres of land they own in St John's Wood are priceless and now they might pay a little more attention to its management – not least in failing on an annual basis to record any trading profits. The impressive list of 'London Spirit' shareholders brings into play a valuable list of potential sponsors for the development of an holistic 'super vision' at Lord's.

Money has rained down on franchise cricket in England, which will now change forever. The starting bid in terms of playing at Lord's was £60m for the 49 per cent of the stake on offer, yet the price in the bidding war rocketed by £3m every 15 minutes. Now the chief executives of Microsoft and Google, an American sportsman and the richest family in Asia have stakes in the future of English cricket. Gone are the days of the amateur chairman, the amateur committee, all in all the amateur administrators, whether they be well meaning or incompetent.

In this bicentenary year of 2025, the stars are in alignment for the future of Lord's to be securitised and a momentous decision will need to be taken with great care by the MCC members. The arcane management structure in place at Lord's since 1786 is one totally unsuited to the competitive commercial environment of high finance at this crucial juncture. A motley army of well-meaning, unelected MCC volunteers is ill-equipped to decide the future of Lord's cricket ground.

MCC used to enjoy a precious independent voice within the cricket world, but no more. The assumed governor of cricket in this country is the England and Wales Cricket Board (ECB), paradoxically dominating the scene at Lord's and happy if necessary to bite the hand that has fed it since it took over from the Test and County Cricket Board (TCCB) in 1995. MCC has provided subsidised offices for the ECB at Lord's and given more than £100m in member subscriptions this century for the benefit of the ECB 'awarding' major matches to MCC at Lord's. Surely a unique example in business of a freeholder being charged for the use of its land?

An historic MCC general meeting of great significance took place on April 8 1864. It was chaired by Lord Suffield and attended by Lord Sefton, the Earl of Aylesford, the Marquis of Ormonde, Lord Charles Russell, Hon. Spencer Ponsonby, Hon. Robert Grimston and 45 members. The estimable RA Fitzgerald, the first professional club secretary, was responsible for the administration of MCC and his industry was largely responsible for bringing together the necessary ingredients to lay the foundations of a permanent future for MCC at Lord's ground.

He had brought the necessary information to appraise members of the facts they needed to address the two resolutions on the agenda: 1) to extend the Lord's lease to 99 years and 2) to open a subscription to raise the required funds from MCC members and the public. 'The committee were of the opinion that they should take early steps for themselves and their successors to secure that place which had always been considered to be the headquarters of cricket, where laws could be made to the advantage of all cricketing classes in the UK.' Lord's ground was recognised to be a highly lucrative property and Fitzgerald commented that many MCC members were completely unaware of the rather important situation they faced in having no right nor title whatsoever to it. The meeting was held to ensure all members could make a fully informed decision following the purchase of Lord's ground four years earlier by Moses and Dark.

What is also noticeable is the humility displayed by the aristocratic committee 'who asked the club members to repose the necessary confidence in the committee that would leave them to take the necessary measures as they might deem to be most convenient to raise the sum necessary to carry out the necessary arrangements suggested and report to the members at the anniversary dinner the following month the progress they had made.' There was no doubt then the committee would be able to furnish a glowing account.

Compare this honourable committee behaviour of the past with the numerous committee failures to recognise the sovereignty of the members in seeking their authority to take major decisions in advance of any executive actions today. For example, the executive actions of two chairmen in 2011 and in 2015 delivering seismic shocks on the cancellation of the 'Vision for Lord's' and the failure to complete the incorporation of MCC by Royal Charter.

In 1864 the committee confirmed in spades their recognition and acceptance that they were placed in a position of acting as the trusted agent on behalf of the members with a very clear duty of care.

The rule from which emanates the MCC committee responsibility for 'the entire management of the property at Lord's' (Rule XII) is conditional and became fatally flawed on July 1 2013 when Royal Charter article 4 (c) required structural change to recognise incorporation and the rightful sovereignty of ownership of Lord's ground remaining with the MCC members. MCC is still a private member club and operating alongside an incomplete body corporate (RC article I). Meanwhile, the club remains in an interregnum.

It was Lord Russell whose speech had the greatest impact at the 1864 meeting. He remarked, as possibly the oldest member present, that he had always attended cricket matches at Lord's partly through his love of the game and partly from public spirit, for no game was better calculated to develop the human frame. He looked upon the game of cricket as a patriotic movement and one of national importance. "As the noble chairman said, nothing could be more important to the interests of cricket than that MCC should enjoy the same respect and authority as that of the Jockey Club."

The game of cricket was becoming more popular by the day and new clubs were in existence everywhere. However, Russell feared that it might degenerate into anything but the art form played by their fathers – the 'professors'. He wished to see

MCC established upon a firm foundation from which it could become a court of appeal to decide all matters connected with the game and to regulate without fear or favour the mode in which the game should be played. Such a universal tribunal was wanted when All England and other X1s were playing teams of 22 players. This was doing the game no good at all.

He thought it was high time for MCC to become masters of their ground and the undisputed law makers of the national game of cricket. The meeting finished with the first resolution supported unanimously. The Lord's lease would be extended for the promotion of the national game of cricket and for the maintenance of the principles at Lord's. The second resolution, to open a subscription to raise the required funds from MCC members and the public, was also agreed.

This might well have been the fundamental reason why, many years later, Gubby Allen, one of the foremost figures at Lord's in the 20th century, opposed so strongly a new British cricket board of control being endowed with the unfettered powers of government.

For any MCC member who remains in doubt over the benefactors' actions and the essence of their generosity, there can be no better expression of their wishes than those expressed by Russell. Not only did he express a wish that ALL MCC members should consider themselves the trustees and guardians of the finest traditions and principles of our national GAME of cricket but also at the premier ground at which it should always be played. How can we sleep easily at night in the full knowledge the MCC committee, acting as an agent, could be said to have erred and strayed from these objectives like lost sheep? Fitzgerald's words spoken as the secretary in 1864 ring so true today: "Many MCC members were (are) completely unaware of the rather important situation they face of having no (obvious) right nor title whatsoever to Lord's ground."

And now for what some readers may consider to be semantics and the difference between playing the 'game of cricket' and the 'sport of cricket.' For me this is the difference between chalk and cheese and the fact is that the MCC committee still has a duty of care whereby the future security of Lord's ground is concerned. That there is no trust deed to be found in the MCC archives does not remove the expression of wishes so clearly recorded in the minutes of the 1864 meeting, unanimously supported by all and sundry at the time.

There can be little doubt that once the traditional MCC laws of the game, domiciled at Lord's, are threatened or traduced, the committee will have a duty of care concerning their preservation. I would suggest that red ball cricket in the form of Tests and other first-class cricket is what should be played in perpetuity at the home of our traditional national game. The latest franchise taster of London Spirit offered by the ECB should be rejected without the need for an unconditional sgm. This is a cricket bastard in every sense.

The ECB should take its franchise business elsewhere and MCC should break out of a suffocating noose at Lord's. Has no member considered the fact that the committee, which oversees the executive management, is associated with an uninterrupted run of trading losses at Lord's ever since it failed to purchase the disused tunnels from Railtrack at the Nursery End in 1999? More evidence is apparent concerning the contract errors over the rebuilding of the Tavern and Allen Stands. The committee's intention to hold an sgm to seek member approval in the absence of any valid contract or funding in place is nugatory for the time being. The time is overdue to remove the committee managing the Lord's estate as the members' agent and retrieve member ownership of Lord's as one body corporate, the members being the rightful share-holders.

The ECB's drawback is that it is a sporting body with no property interests unlike, say, the Jockey Club, the Football Association and the Rugby Football Union. Perhaps its future income should be earned from franchise cricket and building itself a suitable 'Sloggit Stadium' away from Lord's? One thing is certain: the ECB is no longer fit for the purpose of governing English cricket and it is time to recalibrate its role as a manager/administrator with no lawful mandate being granted to govern or control the use of Lord's without the express consent to the conditions of use approved by the MCC members themselves.

There is a single solution: create Lord's ground as a plc owned by the shareholders, the 18,000 members, and managed by a properly qualified team of well-remunerated commercial directors. At a stroke the atmosphere of the committee room, with its carefully chosen volunteers, would be improved by a commercial engine room within a modern suite of offices populated by far-sighted commercial executives charged with the responsibility of releasing the priceless advantages of the ownership of Lord's. This is an opportunity too good to miss.

Committee members give of their time unpaid, apart from the ceo. However, I once asked Dennis Silk, who was then MCC's president and with whom I got on well, if he charged expenses. "Of course," he replied. "Well, I don't," I told him. His response was: "You can afford not to do so." And yet he would have been on a decent ex-warden's (ex-headmaster of Radley College) pension.

Not only can the lost investment of many millions of pounds of member subscriptions be recovered from the disastrous curtailment of the 'Vision at Lord's' in 2011 but monetising the ground itself will energise and enthuse the 18,000 shareholders to create at Lord's a Marylebone Cricket Citadel. This peerless and unchallenged world-class heritage centre of English cricket would embody the finest traditions and spirit of the game, distilled and played by international teams.

The metamorphosis of MCC from a microcosm of society to a macrocosm of society will be a suitable memorial to Ward and his long journey to prevent residential development upon our great ground. It should be preserved by MCC in perpetuity. This is not a revolutionary change but part of a natural conversion from a sleepy member cricket club to a dynamic Royal Charter Corporation.

I venture to suggest that if MCC members were to become Lord's shareholders they would be stimulated. I cannot believe the status quo and the bloated bureaucracy would last ten minutes. The MCC committee has provided jobs for the boys and little else. Lord's deserves better, and member shareholdings would ensure that the ground itself could never be traded to become anything else but the finest cricket venue in the world. Member subscriptions would be replaced by shareholder benefits and dividends.

The MCC committee commissioned a counsel's opinion on the club's future structure from Robert Bramwell QC, who submitted his advice on September 22 2006. He concluded:

> "MCC is an unincorporated association and this would be wound up pursuant to a resolution for reconstruction. The broad objective is to separate the property from the operational interests. The means of division is the creation of two new companies limited by guarantee with membership interests corresponding to the present membership of MCC. The companies are referred to respectively as 'MCC Property' and 'MCC Commercial.'
>
> The principal transfers will include
> A) freehold and the occupational lease of the cricket ground to MCC Commercial with the portfolio of investments
> B) the head lease of the cricket ground to MCC Property together with the non-cricket ground land interests."

Subsequently, the mechanism for this MCC restructuring process was born on December 12 2012 – the Royal Charter.

On August 21 2018 Guy Lavender, secretary and chief executive of MCC, sent me a letter.

Dear Nigel,

The change of club governance from an unincorporated members' association into a Royal Charter Corporation supersedes the past.

Yours sincerely,
GW Lavender

It seems that even MCC's chief executive failed to recognise the problem with the unincorporated members' association remaining extant today.

*

The last 25 years of committee mismanagement have yielded disastrous commercial results. Annual subscriptions have amounted to £173m. A trading deficit of £100m equates to a similar sum paid by MCC to the ECB for staging big matches at Lord's. Operating losses exceeded the total income (including subscriptions) in 2005, 2010, 2011 and 2019.

Catering losses in 2020-2022 were £4.3m and the profit margin in 2023 was reduced to 11 per cent of catering turnover from an average of 30 per cent in previous years. No formal investigation has ever been carried out by the MCC committee. The only year recording a surplus in the last 25 years was in 2021 and that included life memberships of £7.7 million.

As long ago as 1984 a working party drew attention to serious shortcomings in the commercial affairs at Lord's and that MCC was not being run efficiently. In my paper to the members' liaison group dated October 1999 I emphasised the importance of Patrick Milmo QC advising the committee in 1986 that all commercial negotiations on the use of Lord's by any third party should be negotiated at arm's length in the absence of any conflict of interest. I employed counsel to advise. James Findlay QC stressed that "the MCC committee is to exercise a duty of care at all times by acting as the agent in the best interest of

MCC members." The appointed chairman at general meetings had to ensure they acted impartially and Sir Scott Baker "considered that proxy voting seems a fairer system." It has never been utilised.

The liaison group prescribed 'A proper commercial approach to the running of MCC and contractual relationships established with third parties seeking to stage matches at Lord's.' It is bizarre to permit a third party to stage matches at Lord's and expect the freeholders of the land to pay a rental.

The capital costs of maintaining Lord's as a world-class cricket ground have never delivered a market return on the significant member investment. All match bidding is kept secret and MCC members are rarely consulted.

What has been striking in the management of MCC is the preponderance of fellow Cambridge graduates. In particular, the relationship of Silk (chairman of the ECB as well as a former MCC president) following Raman Subba Row (chairman of the Test and County Cricket Board, the governing body's predecessor). George Mann also occupied similar roles. Silk's conflict of interest had an unfortunate repercussion in as much as he failed to ensure the new ECB was made to operate within the confines of a cricket constitution. There can be no good reason for preserving a decrepit MCC management model designed for a private member cricket club that has become a Royal Charter Corporation.

There is today a sad lack of continuity in preserving MCC's history and maintaining its precious traditions. This decay seemed to begin in August 1937 with the creation of a custodian trustee. The remaining managing trustees had a duty of care which has either been ignored or forgotten. This has resulted in a failure in democratic governance. The original five MCC trustees (the Earls of Dudley, Sefton, Bessborough, RJP Broughton and Nicholson) gave a combined lifetime service of 176 years with an average 35 years per trustee. The club minutes of 1865 record their '*names as a sufficient guarantee for the future welfare and prosperity of the club.*' They were the continuity of MCC, but sadly no longer. Today's trustees have no effective powers over ground redevelopment, as was the case in the rules of 1999, save a highly deceptive appellate title, whilst the unhealthy powers of committee dictatorship have gathered in strength. Is this pure coincidence?

Interestingly, had those club rules continued in practice, the arbitrary actions of Oliver Stocken and Justin Dowley, respectively chairman and treasurer, would never, in 2011, have terminated the 'Vision for Lord's,' which would have been funded through development at the Nursery End of the ground.

Rule 14.5 (c)(ii) prior to 2004 read: 'Any development of any freehold or leasehold property or land of the club which in the opinion of the trustees is significant in terms of appearance, cost, or its effect on the amenities or finances of the club, the trustees shall require the committee to convene a general meeting either

Oliver Stocken crashed the Vision for Lord's on the basis there was financial risk to MCC. Oliver Stocken misled the MCC membership as there was no financial risk. This was the developer Almacantar's risk whose shareholders were Chanel, Rolex and Agnelli

to seek approval for the action proposed or to obtain delegation of the powowers of the members in general meeting or to seek the ratification of action taken in urgent or exceptional circumstances by the committee with the consent of the trustees.'

A serious question arises – why did the rewriting of the rules in 2004 remove these significant trustee powers? A new rule 16.7(i) Powers and Duties read: 'When referred to them (the trustees) by the MCC committee.' In other words, the new rules removed the independent sovereignty of the trustees. At a stroke all of the managing trustee powers of 1937 were removed and transferred under rule 13.3 to the committee

The minutes of the 2004 annual meeting record Judge Mackintosh stating *'The New rules transfer more power to the committee.'*

I stated in response: "Following the Sir Scott Baker Structure Review Working Party, the MCC committee promised his members' charter would be included in the new rules as a preamble. In addition, Sir Scott stated that proxy voting was a much fairer system than the postal ballot when the

Justin Dowley, treasurer of MCC aligned himself with Oliver Stocken who took exception to the Vision for Lord's. And the presumption by others was that Justin Dowley would continue the abandonment of the Vision for Lord's.

chairman enjoyed the necessary flexibility to reflect the mood of the meeting." Despite these objections, the new rules were approved by 3,380 votes to 59 against, or 19 per cent support from the total membership. There is little doubt in my mind that the removal of the traditional duties of the trustees from the centre stage of future development at Lord's gave the committee total control of any future development. What had changed to warrant the new trustee rule after 160 years: the arrival of Charles Rifkind as a Lord's freeholder perhaps? There is little doubting the disappointment expressed within the committee room the day after the Railtrack auction on December 10 1999, when he secured the head lease on the disused railway tunnels under the Nursery ground through outbidding MCC.

The French have an aphorism: *Ne jamais deux sans trois* – meaning events happen in threes. Charlie Sale's *The Covers are Off,* published in 2021, was followed in 2024 by Keith

Charlie Sale of the Daily Mail with his book on MCC

Bradshaw's *An Outsider at Lord's*. Now we have the third recent book on Marylebone Cricket Club, written by me. I have decided to call it *Tunnel Vision at Lord's* for reasons which, I hope, will become clear.

My inside knowledge of MCC affairs since I became an elected playing member in 1966 is, I like to think, unequalled. Much of this has been acquired from being a committee-appointed member of six working parties beginning with the Lord Griffiths WP in1993 set up to advise on replacing the dysfunctional Test and County Cricket Board.

Cricket has given me the most amazing experiences of sport, whereby you win or lose gracefully. I feel strongly that Lord's is a special place and it is up to us, members, spectators and enthusiasts, to look after it for future generations. I have no time at all for the people who use the club and the ground for their own selfish interests. I have never had any wish to sit on the main committee. Lord's is, or should be, a venue for the benefit of the nation. I have long thought it was not being properly managed.

'The Covers Are Off' and 'An Outsider at Lord's' dominate the escalator at St John's Wood tube station

I speak from the heart. I am not seeking personal gain from this book nor am I imposing views concerning what the future should hold in NW8. Serving, whether to one's club or one's country, should be an honour. As young doctors and dentists we were brought up in Guy's Hospital in London with a concept of giving. It was one of service within the Guy's motto Dare quam Accipere.

It is a sad fact that since 1968 and the arrival of a political decree removing MCC from the government of our national summer game, this once world-renowned cricket club is only a shadow of its former self. The club once considered a macrocosm of society is certainly not that today.

MCC cricket teams used to be synonymous the world over as the representatives of England with the club organising and financing overseas tours, a practice which ended with the 1976-77 tour of India. This unfortunate loss of status, both within the game of cricket and farther afield, is a story of lost opportunities and the lure of mammon within the Grace Gates. In 2008 this materialised with the appearance of Allen Stanford,

Nigel Knott bowling at Lord's Army v Royal Navy in August 1966

a Texan businessman based in Antigua who arrived at Lord's by helicopter – truly a bizarre event.

Stanford, encouraged by the ECB (as the governing body was now called) had flown in to sign a lucrative Twenty20 contract to stage an international tournament between England and West Indies. He presented Giles Clarke, the chairman of the ECB, with a suitcase (seemingly) full of dollars. (This turned out to be illusory). To say that the reaction of Keith Bradshaw, the new Australian MCC secretary and ceo, was one of shock would be an understatement. Stanford was to be unmasked as a fraudster, the 'Stanford Series' of matches aborted and he was sentenced in 2012 to serve 110 years in an American jail.

Other seminal events since the bicentennial year of 1987 included the rejection of the annual report and accounts that year for the first time in the club's history; the replacement of the TCCB by the ECB in 1997; the admission of female members in 1998; the rejection of the report and accounts for a second time in 1999; the loss of freehold property within the Lord's estate at auction later that year; the creation of the positions of club chairman and chief executive in 2000; the loss of free-to-air TV in 2005 and the Incorporation of MCC by Royal Charter in 2013.

These were at times the product of management failures within the club. The increased risk of IRA terrorist activity in England in the 1970s and subsequent other forms of terrorism prompted concerns within many UK sporting organisations – none more so than MCC, a private members club. A chairman, of MCC, Charles Fry, raised the specific issue of members carrying an unlimited liability in 2006 in the event of a catastrophic financial claim. This liability was removed in 2013 through the grant of a Royal Charter.

The Griffiths working party on which I sat on for a year from 1993 came about because the club had suffered the first rejection of its accounts in history in 1987 – 200 years after its formation. Colin Cowdrey, the then president of MCC (seemingly an appropriate choice in that he had been christened with the initials of the club) and Raman Subba Row, the chairman of the TCCB, had decided that Lord's, which was owned by MCC members, should be used free of charge for international matches. The annual meeting broke up in acrimony and disarray. Jack Bailey, the then secretary of MCC who was protective of members' rights, had already been sacked.

Hence I proposed the formation of what became the Griffiths WP, recommending that we should restructure the government and administration of English cricket: MCC would run the amateur GAME and the TCCB would manage the professional SPORT. The report we produced in 1994 was, I believe, one of great clarity.

I was also appointed, in 2011, to the Incorporation and Structure Working Party (ISWP) under the leadership of Peter Leaver QC. I knew him as a fellow cricketer. I found him authoritarian, self-opinionated – he said to me: 'I'd rather have you inside the tent, pissing outside, not outside pissing in,' which was fair enough. He thought Oliver Stocken, the former treasurer who by now was chairman, a fantastic individual. This seminal body recommended a method (Royal Charter) whereby members could have their unlimited liability removed at a stroke. Hitherto, had a bomb gone off, members would have had an unlimited liability concerning a claim of a catastrophic nature.

A Royal Charter had been granted in 2012. In 2015 the ISWP completed the second phase of its work by making 27 recommendations for the reform of the structure and governance of MCC in line with its obligations as a Royal Charter Corporation. More than a decade later, the constitutional reform process is incomplete, just as the 'Vision for Lord's' redevelopment remained incomplete when it was aborted in 2011. Although there is buildings insurance in place, the Lord's estate today remains vulnerable to an unlimited liability claim.

There is uncertainty and the law does not tolerate this. Uncertainty remains and the hidden consequences are serious in that the ownership of Lord's cricket ground remains exposed. The summary disbandment of the ISWP, before its task was complete, was history being repeated.

Today, the Lord's estate is recorded as being in the sole proprietorship of Marylebone Cricket Club at His Majesty's Land Registry and was registered as such in December 2020. No reference is made to the fact that a parcel of land within the Lord's Estate is owned by a property developer in Rifkind. Efforts to redress this extraordinary failure to create one body corporate, MCC have been ignored, raising the suspicion that something is rotten in the State of Denmark (Lord's). The admission in 2024 of 'irregularities' discovered in the club accounts, in addition to huge catering losses over two years, although this did include the Covid period, gave rise to further rumour and suspicion.

My objections over governance have not gone down well with the hierarchy. I objected to Michael Melluish, the then MCC treasurer, becoming a trustee in 1999, as in my view the two roles should be separate from each other. He was behind all the discussions over charging members for entry to Lord's to watch World Cup matches in 1999, with which I disagreed. "I'm going to ensure you never get onto the main committee," he told me. Tim Rice, the lyricist who also became a trustee, strongly objected to what I had to say a few years later about the proposed installation of floodlights. I felt the objection of residents living near the ground should be taken into account and I was concerned also about the proliferation of white ball matches. Robin Marlar, the then president, failed to protect me. I had several attempts to join the main committee – the nearest I came was 137 votes short. Out of eight candidates for four places, I came fifth and Philip Hodson, who subsequently became president, was last. Melluish by then had stood down, but as I have mentioned, this was not a position I ever especially desired

MCC remains in an extraordinary state of disorganised government. The ISWP report, which took more than four years to (semi) complete, included professional advice from the accountants Price Waterhouse Cooper and the solicitors Freshfields and Farrer & Co, whose counsel's opinion concerning the future security of Lord's remains unheeded. 'The MCC committee is responsible for the entire management of the property, funds and affairs of the club' (rule13.1). And it is stated (rule 31) that "The committee shall have the power to decide all questions arising in respect of (the) interpretation of these rules and regulations.' Democracy or dictatorship?

MARYLEBONE CRICKET CLUB
Annual Report and Accounts 1999

MCC Committee 1999-2000

Back Row: R.G. Marlar, M.O.C. Sturt, J.A.F. Vallance, N.M. Peters, J.A. Bailey, Sir Timothy Rice, O.H.J. Stocken, D.A. Peck, T.J.G. O'Gorman
Middle Row: Lord Alexander of Weedon, E.R. Dexter, M.J. de Rohan, C.A. Fry, R.P. Hodson, B.A. Sharp, A.W. Wreford
Front Row: R.D.V. Knight, D.L. Hudd, Sir Michael Jenkins, A.R. Lewis, D.R.W. Silk, Lord Cowdrey of Tonbridge, M.E.L. Melluish
Absent: D.J.C. Faber, T.M.B. Sissons

The MCC Tunnel Vision Committee

David Batts, MCC's assistant secretary who oversaw the 'Vision for Lord's'

*Simon Elliot, brother-in-law of the Queen Consort
and adviser to Charles Rifkind on the 'Vision for Lord's'*

Robert Griffiths KC, chairman of MCC's development committee who clashed with the club's hierarchy

David Morley (left), architect, and John Dyke, consultant, on the 'Vision for Lord's'

Warloy-Baillon Communal Cemetery Extension where Lt SJG Knott is buried
Image Courtesy of Commonwealth War Graves Commission

Chapter 1 – A Warrior Family
Paying the ultimate price of service

Chapter 1
A Warrior Family

Cricket had always been my prime sporting enthusiasm. My father, James Knott, came from a brewing family on the Isle of Wight and my mother, Claire Henriette McInerny, was a qualified cordon bleu cook whose family were French. There were no sportsmen or women or sporting talent in my family. My great grandfather, William Knott, was the owner of a brewery in Newport on the island. My grandfather, Sydney, married into the Cheverton family, who could trace their lineage back to William the Conqueror.

An extraordinary piece of family history is documented in the Cheverton family tree of Chiverton of Chiverton wherein the first recorded family antecedent is William, 1st count of Chievres, 'a companion of William the Conqueror in 1066.' Chievres is a district in the province of Hainaut in Belgium. It was part of the German occupation in World War I until liberated in 1918 by the 5th Battalion Gordon Highlanders. Two years previously, my grandfather was killed whilst serving as an officer in 3rd. Battalion Worcestershire Regiment, fighting on the Somme with 1st Battalion Wiltshire Regiment to defeat the German military occupation of France and Belgium.

His posting as an officer to the Third Army was ordered on May 29 1916. "You will proceed to join your unit by the train leaving at 4:10 pm." He was killed in action on July 8 that year in an attack on the German trenches, supporting the Wiltshire Regiment. This was a significant action, marked by the following despatch sent by the general officer commanding 25th Division on July 17 1916: "I wish to congratulate the 1st Battalion Wiltshire Regiment and 3rd Battalion Worcestershire Regiment on their gallant behaviour during the operations that took place between the 6th and 8th of July 1916. During this period the 1st Battalion Wiltshire Regiment carried out three attacks, repelled several determined counter-attacks on two consecutive nights and firmly held the position won under an intense bombardment which lasted over four hours."

German counter-attacks delivered during the night of July 7 were easily repulsed with heavy enemy losses. At 6:30 am on July 8 a second Wiltshire Regiment attack was launched. The moment the men appeared over the parapet they were met with overwhelming fire from machine-guns and rifles, but despite their many casualties they pressed on and by 9:30 hrs the heavily fortified communications trench that was their objective was captured and consolidated. This performance was all the more creditable given the truly awful weather conditions and the ground being cut up by shell fire, with the troops fatigued by 36 hours of combat. As the attacking troops reached the enemy's trench, the Germans were seen to bolt. Large numbers were killed and 23 prisoners taken. 2/Lt Clegg was the only officer left alive. He was wounded and showed conspicuous courage in consolidating the captured trench under heavy bombardment.

'The position was held with great determination but the situation was now critical and had to be reinforced by two companies from 3rd Worcestershire Regiment. The reinforcements performed with the greatest gallantry and dash. They brought up plenty of ammunition and a large supply of bombs and with their assistance all enemy counter-attacks were easily repelled. None of this success could have been achieved without the heroic courage, stamina and devotion to duty of the officers, ncos and soldiers of the 1st Battalion Wiltshire Regiment and the 3rd. Battalion Worcestershire Regiment, so many of whom have earned undying honour by giving their lives in the country's cause.'

My grandfather's personal belongings included a letter written by his seven year-old son dated June 4 1916. "Dear Daddy, How are you getting on?' I hope you are quite well and will write to me when you get this. We will send you some chocklots. Love from Jimmy."

Frank Cheverton, the brother of Jimmy's widowed mother, paid for all his school fees at Cranleigh and his training at Guy's Hospital, a wonderful act of benevolence. In the family tree we find Sir Richard Cheverton, a prominent member of the Worshipful Company of Skinners (granted a Royal Charter in1327) and one of the great 12 livery companies in the City of London, becoming Lord Mayor of London from 1657-1658. This may explain how he came to be knighted in 1658 by Oliver Cromwell, which was followed in 1663 with a further knighthood, this time by Charles II. A very successful balancing act of diplomacy. He died on November 25 1679 and was buried at Clerkenwell.

Twenty-five years after my grandfather's death in France, the father of my wife Rosemary, Lewin Hepworth was killed serving with the Eighth Army at El-Alamein two weeks before she was born on June 6 1941. The fateful news was conveyed in a letter from his company commander in the 38th Light Anti-Aircraft Battery RA. His emotional message included details of the carnage following an arial attack from a Heinkel bomber and the hurried memorial ceremony to bury the dead. "His grave is about 200 yards inside the wire separating Egypt from Libya. The nearest place is Carpuzzo. The grave was marked with a cross and the particulars sent to the proper authorities of its location. Unfortunately, I was unable to take a photograph as we had to vacate our position with some rapidity."

When I had left the army, I moved with my family to live in Ratford Farmhouse within a small settlement near Calne, Wiltshire. Some years later we experienced a 'small world incident' when Rosemary, my wife and I were invited to dinner at Bremhill Manor by Oliver and Jane Clegg, who also owned the Manor Hotel at Castle Combe. Rosemary sat between Oliver Clegg and Lord Goodman. Oliver announced he was going to revisit Sheffield at the weekend for an old comrades reunion. This immediately sharpened Rosemary's attention as her family roots were in Ecclesall Road, Sheffield. She asked him: "Did you know Lewin Hepworth?" He paused and he replied: "Yes I did – we served in the same Regiment RA during World War II," to which Rosemary answered with amazement; "He was my father who was killed in Egypt before I was born." Lewin was a keen cricketer working in the Sheffield banking sector before wartime service.

*

I was educated at Highgate in north London, where, it is fair to say, my main interests did not incorporate my academic studies. Representing the school at cricket and Eton fives was on my list of achievements, topped only perhaps by being promoted to company sergeant major in the Combined Cadet Force. Yet I was the sole pupil among my contemporaries not to enjoy the authority of being a school monitor. And the CCF promotion was based on merit!

I could never have imagined that a love of the game and the hero worship of Denis Compton and Fred Trueman would lead me to playing at Lord's and many years later having a significant role in gaining a Royal Charter for MCC. Maybe it was the tousled black hair of both of these titans that defined their heroic performances on the field of play. Deep inside me was a desire to strike the ball as hard as possible as a batsman and project it at cyclonic speed as an opening bowler.

The first I did achieve at the age of ten at my preparatory school, Norfolk House, against Forest School, through hitting the first five balls one bounce to the boundary. Much later, having been hit for 20 off my first five balls when representing MCC against Winchester College as a playing candidate for the club, I managed to uproot the leg stump of the batsman with the sixth ball of the over. I finished with seven for 35. In another MCC 'qualifier' I claimed the first three wickets at Sherborne School on a very quick pitch and was taken off by Derek Bridge, the MCC captain and the school's cricket master, who promptly lost the game!

My father had been informed a few months before my O levels that I might be suited to a career in banking and should leave school early to make a start. In August 1957 a post card arrived with **'P'** against all my subjects. I had defied long odds by landing an accumulator in racing terms. So I stayed on.

Highgate School CCF 1958 – Nigel Knott Back Row on the right

Maybe banking would have been a better choice after all. My mother had taught domestic science at the Northern Polytechnic in London and her solution was to inform the headmaster that I was to take my A level zoology in one year and then leave school to attend the 'Poly.' Guy's Hospital beckoned – I had decided to study medicine and dentistry – and one year's school fees at Highgate amounting to £90 would be saved by my parents. My career was preordained in a sense: my family connections with Guy's were deep-seated through my father having been appointed house surgeon to Sir William Kelsey Fry, a renowned surgeon, in 1932.

My wife, Rosemary, also qualified at Guy's as a state registered nurse and her Aunt Barbara qualified at Guy's as a midwife in the early 1930s, at the same time as my father. Having joined the Commonwealth Nursing Service and being posted to Ipoh Hospital in Malaysia a few years later, Barbara somehow managed to survive the war years in Changi Jail in Singapore during the Japanese occupation. Twenty-two years later I was posted to the British Military Hospital in Kluang, Malaysia, to serve with the Brigade of Gurkhas – a privilege, with plenty of cricketing opportunities through representing the army and West Malaysia on an interesting variety of pitches in tropical conditions. I recall once playing in an all-day match in Singapore on a flooded ground which was fit for play again within four hours.

Leaving school one year early brought an amazing feeling of freedom within a new learning environment whereby self-discipline and adulthood were moulded in a truly multicultural environment. And the standard of cricket was excellent at Guy's. The cricket X1, which I was to captain in due course, included four current or future county players. I enjoyed the finest training in medicine and dentistry that anyone could have wished for and managed to be selected to play for United Hospitals XI against Surrey 2nd XI at the Oval in 1962.

The year of 1966 proved to be eventful. After leaving Guy's I joined the army as a dental officer. The cricket fixture list was one attraction. I had the incredible experience of opening their bowling at Lord's – a privilege to be repeated on another four occasions that included representing Combined Services. The date of my debut at headquarters, on August 19, was within three days of a landmark in MCC's history: the centenary of the ownership of Lord's cricket ground.

Two months later, in October 1966, I was caught up in one of the most tragic events of recent times: the Aberfan disaster, which occurred when a colliery spoil tip collapsed, resulted in 144 people losing their lives. I was part of the emergency army support team from the King's Own Royal Border Regiment summoned from Heathfield Camp in Honiton to the nightmare scene. The death toll finally amounted to 116 children from Pant Glas School, Merthyr Tydfil, and 28 adults.

Soon after my arrival at the scene I received a call from the Regional Crime Squad for assistance with the harrowing task of resolving the unknown identity of a child. The problem facing the police was the refusal of two parents to recognise a dead child's identity. They were in a state of total shock. What an absolute nightmare confronted us. I began by contacting the Community Dental Service to access the school's dental records while at the same time requesting the distressed parents to supply us with recent photographs of their child exposing his teeth in a happy smile.

The results proved my hunch of a mistaken identity. The dead child's dental records did not match the photographic images of the anterior (the top front teeth). We were fortunate in being able to age the child with two unerupted incisor teeth clearly marked as being present on the dental records but we were now faced with a major problem. The identity process had to be revisited but where could we begin? One of the police officers pointed out a parent with a handkerchief over her face attempting to stem the flow of tears. Luck was on our side as we asked the distressed couple if they recognised this child – they did. It was theirs.

What a relief to return home to find my wife and young son

safe and sound. I was to revisit, more than 50 years later, the wonderful and serenely peaceful Aberfan Memorial Gardens.

In 1970 I was posted to a Gurkha regiment in Penang (1/10 PMO Gurkha Rifles) which included the only serving Victoria Cross holder, L/Cpl Rambahdur Limbu. The cricket moved up in class as the Penang Sports Club possessed a high-class turf square and competitive fixture lists which included matches against strong Australian touring teams. However, a wonderful tour of duty with Gurkha regiments and at the British Military Hospital, where I was working in the dental department for 18 months, was moving to a close and my return to the UK meant an unexpected emergency posting to serve with 1st Battalion Parachute Regiment in Belfast, Northern Ireland, soon afterwards, in December 1971. A short posting that proved eventful, to say the least.

Soon after my arrival at Hollywood Barracks, Belfast, the battalion was placed on standby as troubles erupted in Londonderry – a 'no-go' area that gave rise to the infamous 'Bloody Sunday' episode. One evening, upon returning late to the mess with three other officers, we were stopped by the Royal Military Police at the camp entrance to have our car searched. They explained there had been an incident at the mess. The IRA had blown a large hole in the outside wall of my bedroom with 20lbs of semtex. Another nearby bomb, also semtex 'made in the Republic of Ireland' failed to explode six minutes later as the force of the explosion had stopped the timing mechanism. A narrow escape. I could well have been killed had I been inside.

On arriving back in the officers mess bar I was informed the catering corps cook had absconded and was suspected of being part of an internal IRA cell. He disappeared to his home in southern Ireland and later emigrated to the United States where he was sheltered from any attempted murder charges – but why bomb my bedroom before deserting?

One officer comedian decided it was the obvious place to target as I had voiced my disapproval the previous evening about the lousy dinner we had eaten. More plausible was the fact I had drawn the curtains and left a table lamp on, so that it appeared from the outside I was sitting at the bedside table. Adjoining my room was the back entrance to the mess with little or no outside lighting and some bushes nearby – an ideal bomb site.

A news blackout and curfew were imposed immediately and the adjutant, Captain Mike Jackson (later General Jackson) left a message for me to see the commanding officer, Colonel Wilford, first thing in the morning. He informed me that a member of my staff, a corporal, had been followed a few days previously and was seen to leave the camp in the early hours. His home was in Londonderry and he was my driver when visiting the barracks at Ballykinler. We wore plain clothes to avoid the need for an armed escort whilst travelling in uniform.

Colonel Wilford considered the corporal was a security risk and wanted him removed from the barracks soonest. This was no easy task and his departure had to be sanctioned by my own commanding officer stationed at divisional HQ in Lisburn. He arrived the next morning to examine my wrecked bedroom and to be briefed by Colonel Wilford, who asked Colonel Fletcher how rapidly the corporal could be returned to Aldershot. He responded "within a month" to which Colonel Wilford replied: "I am thinking about 24 hours." Immediately afterwards I had to make a very nervous visit to tell the corporal and his family to pack their bags and prepare to leave in the morning.

Soon after my own return from Belfast and less than one month after the 'Bloody Sunday' crisis, a vast explosion shook the Parachute Regiment officers mess in Aldershot on February 22 1972 that killed six people and injured 19 more. This revenge attack involved an IRA bomb consisting of 280lb of explosive packed into a Ford Cortina that demolished most of the mess building during the lunch break. As I had left a war zone only days previously, the Army Special Investigation Branch was in contact to take a statement from me to record my experience.

The 1st Battalion Parachute Regiment was well-known in

Belfast as a 'no nonsense' battalion and when ordered into the 'no-go' area of Londonderry on January 30 1972 they entered a zone in which IRA snipers were present and who fired the first shots. The fact no para troops were killed or injured was testimony to their training and professionalism. Believe me, carrying a firearm with yellow card instructions on the conditions of use before any weapon can be discharged is quite some responsibility.

I can well understand why so many highly trained police officers today are so reluctant to carry firearms as this responsibility has become far too great.

What still distresses me more than 50 years later is the incredible courage and bravery of so many military personnel on active service in a war zone being questioned in the cosy comfort of the courts to answer criminal charges on suggested war crimes. It defies belief.

*

My annual confidential report arrived soon after I was back at the garrison at Larkhill in Wiltshire to enjoy another summer playing cricket. It reflected the irritation of my commanding officer at being ordered by General (later Field Marshal; a keen cricket enthusiast) Bramall, chairman of the Army Sports Control Board, and later President, MCC, to release me from the dental centre duties to represent the army. "This officer spends too much time playing cricket and not enough time practising dentistry" was the commanding officer's take. Ouch! A strong hint an army career might not be the best choice. I left six months later.

A few months passed before I applied for premature retirement from my happy days within the relatively comfy confines of army service to face the unpredictable challenge of self-employment in NHS dental practice in Wiltshire, where running an old farmhouse and family demands brought an end to my cricketing days. I was to be an associate working within a large conglomerate based in Chippenham, where the senior partner was chairman of Wiltshire Family Practitioner Committee.

It was here I uncovered fraud within the practice. I discovered the NHS EC17 claim for treatment forms were being falsified to include service items not provided for patients. I reported my concerns to the senior partner, who sacked me and then sought a High Court injunction to stop me practising in Wiltshire. My professional indemnity policy should have given me legal expenses cover but failed to do so.

The senior partner, Leslie Barker-Tufft, barked: " I have noticed your unhappy demeanour in recent days and suggest your best solution is to leave my practice forthwith."

Two weeks later I received an injunction served from the Queen's Bench Division, High Court, Bristol. My application for professional indemnity cover from my legal protection insurer was rejected by the secretary, who emphasised that only discretionary cover was offered. The subsequent three-day court case was terminated by Mr Justice Eastham within three hours and costs awarded in my favour

The prosecuting counsel approached me immediately after the trial ended to explain: "I hope you do not have any hard feelings towards me as I wish to tell you l advised my clients not to proceed with this prosecution as they would lose." What a beginning to my civilian life with a wife, a mortgage and three children at private schools to support. Fortunately, my HSBC bank manager, also a keen cricketer, promised to secure overdraft facilities to cover a very difficult period. There was an interesting sequel to this incident following the police referral to the Dental Estimates Board for investigation. The case was referred to the Wiltshire Family Practitioner Committee for disciplinary action when Mr. Barker-Tufft was chairman – doctor heal thyself! I have no knowledge of any disciplinary proceedings being taken.

As my family and my career were now my priority, it was not

until 16 years later, when I attended the MCC annual meeting of 1987, that the game, and indeed the club, took centre stage. It was John Reason, the outspoken *Sunday Telegraph* reporter, who sounded the alarm with a back page piece in early May headlined 'Cuckoo in the Lord's Nest.' What a stark warning! Sadly, that cuckoo is still domiciled at Lord's in a bigger and fatter format. It is dressed in the garb of the ECB.

Sir Stephen Fry with his sister, Jo, and Philip Johnston, deputy editor of the Daily Telegraph (right) in the president's box at Lord's. In the author's estimation, Fry was the worst president in MCC's history.

*Malcolm Le May (left) a significant supporter of the
'Vision for Lord's' with Nigel Knott*

Mike Morgan, an MCC member intent on change

Mike Milton, who along with Mike Morgan has held MCC to account over various issues

Nigel Knott, the author

Lord Grabiner KC, who sat on MCC's development committee

"So your membership finally came through?"

Chapter 2 – A Club in Conflict
The end of an independent cricket government

Chapter 2
A Club in Conflict

The summary removal of MCC as the governing body of English cricket in 1968 was not unexpected as having a private members club in charge of a national game and sport was anachronistic. However, in retrospect, this transformational milestone proved to be the slippery slope into a slough of despond with persistent internecine strife within the club and constant friction with the newly created TCCB and its successor, the ECB. An unknown number of MCC sticking plaster working parties (WPs) have come and gone; many with sensible recommendations being ignored or rejected by an all-powerful MCC committee. Two of the six I sat on between 1992 and 2015 were disbanded without being allowed to report to members. These were the Staging Agreement WP and the Members Liaison WP. The committee interference amounted to a waste of everyone's time.

More than a decade has elapsed since the club was granted Royal Charter status in 2012 and still little or no evidence of a democratically governed club exists. Indeed, Rule XI of 1867 is still extant more than 150 years later – 'The MCC committee shall be responsible for the entire (day to day) management of the property, funds and everyday affairs of the club.' This is probably why the club has acquired a public perception as being old-fashioned and completely out of touch.

Perhaps the greatest and most damaging effect has been the change in character and composition of the MCC membership from a 'Cricketer Club,' as it was known, to a cheque book club of 'chums.' The annual report of 1875 tells a tale: 'It is much to be lamented that the playing strength of the club does not appear to have advanced in due proportion to the increased roll of members.' By 1900 the rules demanded that out of 120 new members each year, 80 had to be properly qualified cricketers with a commitment to play as many matches for the club as possible. A failure to appear regularly on the field of play would be sanctioned with a return to the waiting list of candidates and a lengthy wait to rejoin.

The club today has more than 90 percent of members as 'waiters' (elected non-playing members) and all of us (including elected playing members) are described as 'ordinary members' in the club rules. On being elected a playing member in 1966 I was required to give an assurance to represent the club on the field of play in future whenever possible.

My story of Lord's and MCC, beginning with the purchase of the freehold land (Lord's) in August 1866, moves on rapidly to the events that begin with the seminal defeat of the MCC committee at the bicentenary annual meeting of May 6 1987 – for the first time in the club's history – and the subsequent issues. The committee's lack of perspicuity and cavalier inattention to member communications was a wake-up call for ordinary members like myself to take a greater interest in club affairs, beginning the long journey of attempting to deliver the necessary reform and the preservation and protection of members' rights and privileges at Lord's. This was to prevent members still being treated as children – to be seen but not heard. Naughty schoolboys like me are either disciplined or sent to Coventry.

The 1987 meeting was followed soon afterwards by my attempt to set up an MCC enquiry. My personal correspondence with the president, Dennis Silk, resulted in the Griffiths WP being formed.

English cricket was going through a difficult period when Silk became president of MCC in 1992. He had captained

Cambridge University in 1955, having scored centuries against Oxford University in the previous two seasons and went on to play for Somerset. He was exceptionally popular as the warden of Radley College and his easy-going and urbane manner singled him out for the presidency. Silk admitted to me when he became chairman of the TCCB in 1994 that his attempt to balance the interests of conflicting bodies had become difficult in the extreme.

In 1999 further ructions became apparent and an equally contentious annual meeting ended prematurely with Tony Lewis, the then president, announcing: "I am fed up with this member disruption and I am adjourning this agm to go and enjoy a few glasses of claret at the annual dinner." It is notable these two member rebellions were about a single fundamental principle which the committee failed (and still fails) to recognise – the sovereignty of member rights and privileges. In 1999 these concerned additional entry fees for World Cup fixtures. The committee, supported by the president, wanted the members to pay to watch matches on the ground they owned. No doubt many of them – us – would have acquiesced to this had they been consulted initially.

I wrote to Lewis, pointing out that he had been left floundering at the agm.

> 'I felt that your initiative (he had set up a members' liaison group) was at least a constructive way forward. But no, the dinosaurs always know best (only one had the courtesy to reply to my letter to all committee members in an attempt to gain their support for you.) I hope that you do not intend to tell members that we have agreed to your course of action, which is patently not the case. There are a number of other serious inaccuracies in the last minutes (which appear to have been heavily edited) including the fact that the secretary used the word 'unconstitutional' to describe your action (do you recall

our meeting with him at Lord's in April when this idea was first discussed?)

'Neither is it reported that I stated the secretary was talking rot (euphemistically speaking) and it was quite within the president's remit to set up an advisory group if he so desired and I also felt that if the committee failed to back him they were being disloyal. There are some other pretty serious omissions – how about my question about the secretary's financial package and the reply of the chairman, Sir Michael Jenkins, that he would tell me after the meeting? How about my remarks that the MCC website was a complete embarrassment and the fact that I produced at the meeting downloaded images which showed an out-of-date committee. Where is my formal proposal on the way forward for exploiting the commercial value with a totally different team? I have kept notes of the meeting and I am not prepared to accept the draft that I have been sent as an accurate record.

'When are we to be given the opportunity of discussing the minutes of our last meeting. You have a difficult task where the final report is concerned and I am sorry that you did not accept the suggestion that we should meet again to finalise these matters.

I regret causing you further problems as I know that you yourself have made a genuine attempt to resolve matters amicably and honourably. Sadly obstacles are being placed in your way by the darker spirits.'

Best wishes,
Nigel

In fact, things have not improved since. Democratic government of MCC has disappeared completely. There is a disconnection between the executive and the membership – the committee no longer understands it is the agent acting on behalf of the members' best interests. My earnest wish is to bring the attention of members and the public to the decline of an ancient, well-respected institution once enjoying royal patronage, a club owning Lord's but with a very uncertain future. I care passionately about the preservation of the traditional national grass roots amateur game of cricket and in particular retaining Lord's as the world-class HQ of Test match cricket and the permanent home of our national team.

In such a troubled society today, playing games should be a central part of life and cricket has proved through the ages to have a civilising influence across the world. The game itself is increasingly being subjected to secular commercial influences. MCC is, if nothing else. the guardian and bastion (Lord's) of the finest traditions in what remains principally a widely enjoyed amateur game as distinct from a heavily commercialised professional sport barely worthy of the name of cricket.

The deployment of ancient committee power has had an extraordinarily damaging effect within MCC. It is a primary cancer within the body corporate with a massive spread of malignant secondary growths within numerous organs of management activity. I am reminded constantly of my correspondence with the Privy Council Office (PCO) soon after our structure WP consultative green paper was vetoed by a new club chairman, Gerald Corbett, who promised an independent enquiry and my appeal for assistance from the club trustees was ignored. My follow-up telephone call raised the question of MCC not being fit for the purposes of a democratic Royal Charter organisation.

The response was instructive. The Crown had gifted MCC the necessary instrument for change and the last occasion when a Royal Charter was withdrawn was during the Reign of James I. This of course, was reminiscent of Winston Churchill's seminal advice: "And when in subsequent ages, the State swollen with its own authority has attempted to ride roughshod over the rights and liberties of the subject, it is to their doctrine (the rule of law) that appeal has again and again been made, and never as yet been without success."

It was not until the late 1970s that 'proprietary' first appeared in the club rules under 'Dissolution.' Today it is entrenched in Royal Charter article 14. This member proprietorship of Lord's was not in the club rules of 1973 and has appeared mysteriously since that date. It seems to correspond to gradual dissipation and today the complete sterilisation of the powers of the trustees at Lord's. Significant promises from committee members and smooth excuses have been made over the past two decades as to the clearly defined MCC trustee duties and responsibilities to the members. It is my entrenched belief that Lord's cricket ground remains the subject of a trust as per the terms and conditions of the trustee documents dated August 30/31 1937.

Paragraph six of the Scott Baker WP report, which was sent to all members:

> 'We think the present rules are unduly complicated, out of date, poorly drafted and difficult in some

Gerald Corbett, who succeeded Oliver Stocken as Chairman MCC. He played a significant role in vetoing the formation of an elected MCC Members' Committee and in preventing the MCC becoming a properly constituted Royal Charter Corporation. Gerald Corbett promised an independent enquiry regarding the Vision for Lord's; this never happened. Instead he organised an internal review but relied upon his biased document favouring the MCC hierarchy approach.
Gerald Corbett's chairmanship is the root cause of a constitutional crisis

instances to follow. They should be simplified and made more user-friendly. We think they should be completely redrafted by the club's solicitor and they should be updated annually.

'Members' basic rights should be identified in a members' charter which should be spelt out as a preamble to the rules. These rights should be enshrined as part of the rules and should be capable of removal only by a two thirds majority of members voting at a general meeting.

'Other than those rights that form part of the members' charter, any rule ought to be capable of change by a simple majority. In our view the present across-the-board provision requiring a two thirds majority to change any rule is restrictive and undemocratic. Further work is required on the contents of the members' charter. What we envisage is a short statement or series of points setting out the fundamental privileges and obligations of membership.'

Committee comment:

'A members' charter will be produced as a preamble to the rules. Members' benefits and privileges are currently defined in the MCC regulations booklet, but members' obligations will also be included in the charter.

'Rules which become enshrined in the members' charter should be altered or removed only by a two thirds majority of members exercising their right to vote in respect of a resolution proposed at a general meeting. The committee accepts that it would be sensible for other rule changes to be decided by a simple majority. This will be fully considered in the redrafting of the rules.'

The committee never placed the Scott Baker report before the membership for formal adoption at the annual meeting and neither was any opportunity given to the membership to accept or reject their comments on the report either by a show of hands then or by postal ballot. In the memorandum published on January 30 2004 concerning the new rules it is stated 'Rule 2- membership': 'However, in the report of the structure working party it was recommended that a 'members' charter be published and the new rule provides this in the form of a list of the rights of full and senior members.'

The committee dishonoured their assurance given to the membership that a members' charter would be drawn up and enshrined in the new club rules with the necessary protection against fundamental change. No members' charter was ever approved by MCC members and published in the club rules.

On a lighter note, soon after the 1999 agm World Cup ructions, I received a postcard from Michael Parkinson, the broadcaster and cricket enthusiast who had written critically about MCC in the past. I had never met him but he had gleaned what was going on from press reports. 'Dear Nigel, I have to tell you, your reform agenda will come to nought in the absence of the sound of gunfire and the smell of cordite within the Grace Gates. Good luck and best regards MP.'

I submitted the following contribution to the Griffiths WP on July 22 1993 following the resolution approved at the agm to investigate the administration and governance of English cricket.

> 'It is clear from the recently recorded history that the Cricket Council should be abolished and the TCCB responsibility for all aspects of the professional game reviewed. A new constitution should be drawn up with the necessary checks and balances, with above all else, proper transparency and accountability. Good government must be democratic and accountable – neither requirement can be seen to be present in the existing structure which is secretive and protective. Even the more informative MCC annual accounts of 1991 have again been the subject of restriction in 1992 at the request

of the TCCB. Grave concerns have been expressed over the aggressive commercialisation of cricket. We must question the need for the TCCB to be given unfettered financial control over the Test match grounds (TMGs) on big match days.

'Quite obviously the TCCB has to be properly financed and the counties given generous support. I believe we should look at a more satisfactory commercial relationship between the TCCB and each of those TMGs whose assets are the source of the game's income.'

Nigel J Knott Member GWP

It is worth recording the contents of a personal letter written to Lord Griffiths on November 5 1993 in my capacity as a member of his working party, reinforcing my concerns.

'Dear Lord Griffiths,

I hope you will not mind reading some further thoughts I have had since our last meeting. You have done a magnificent job guiding us through the overgrown jungle of cricket administration. Whilst we have now a clear overview and a consensus seems to be emerging, I am concerned by the risk of a last fence fall.

Michael Melluish is right to point out the very real danger of a new British cricket board of control becoming just another all-powerful replica of the TCCB. The concept we have identified so far, is a good one with the first-class and minor counties having the overall responsibility for the organisation and administration in their particular domain of the amateur game. However, the presence at the top of an overall management team that is representative and accountable is an imperative. We should be mindful that the constitution of the Cricket Council during its initial period in government reflected ten votes each for MCC and NCA representing the recreational (amateur) game and five votes for the professional sport.

These numbers were later turned upside down with 13 votes being cast against three for MCC. It seems to me the root cause of most of our present problems, apart from the administrative chaos, arises from the professional and commercial interests being allowed to swamp those of the amateur game for which MCC should be the guardian and trustee. The pendulum has swung too far in the direction of a professional sport and an unfortunate opposition seems to exist towards the amateur game of today.

The role of the great club is still as vital today as the bastion of the traditions and ethics of our wonderful civilising game. Any new structure which will diminish our duty as the guardian of our national game of cricket must be rejected.

It will be ironic, if the initiative begun by Gubby Allen and Billy Griffith to include other interested parties in the future government of cricket in 1968 resulted in an eclipse of MCC 25 years later!

Very best wishes, Nigel Knott.'

Five years later at the 1998 agm I had cause to raise further matters.

'To discuss a matter of which written notice has been given by Dr. N J Knott and A A Meyer in accordance with Rule 21.4(e):

The Griffiths working party in their 1994 report emphasised the importance of a proper constitution for the new English Cricket Board (ECB).

A letter from the ECB dated September 1 1997 states there are no formal contracts in place between the ECB and any of the ground authorities who stage international or indeed other matches under the control of the ECB ... It may well be the case that for the future we may wish to consider more formal arrangements…. However, there are no imminent proposals for this to happen for the routine International or domestic fixtures.'

The transfer of power and authority from the TCCB to the ECB introduces new legal responsibilities which need to be resolved now. In particular, mechanisms have to be identified for consulting MCC members on this new relationship and the introduction of formal contracts at Lord's with the ECB.

It is proposed that the Griffiths working party be re-convened as a matter of urgency to report and recommend to the MCC membership for their approval:

(i) a contractual relationship with the ECB at Lord's which properly protects the rights and privileges of MCC members and

(ii) the future role and responsibilities of MCC in English and world cricket within the framework of the new ECB.'

I then said: "The two parts of this resolution are clearly related and in essence centre on our identity and our place on the field of play. We have in the space of 30 years seen this great club create a new administrative structure for cricket, we have witnessed an unsavoury struggle for power and total control of the game by the few, we have observed the gradual sterilisation of MCC interests and now we experience the naked aggression which frequently accompanies unfettered commercialisation. Can this be in the best interests and the finest traditions of our national game? Are members of this club, who are, after all, contributing a small fortune to the game, prepared to be moved to the boundary in a spectator's role? Are you prepared to be disenfranchised from your rights and privileges at Lord's?"

In my address at the sgm in 1987 I said that the serious issues would not go away and could not be swept under the carpet. There has since been an unwillingness or, more contentiously, a steadfast refusal to tackle our problems. There has been a period of obfuscation and fudge. I drew attention that year to the fact that MCC members had a right to enter their own ground on production of a member pass without payment other than their subscription for that privilege and without payment being made by the club on their behalf. This member right was confirmed at the agm in 1984 and is confirmed in the 1998 regulations. It has in fact been ignored since.

When he was president, Colin Cowdrey wrote to all MCC members before the agm in 1987: "If responsibilities were exercised in a way that seriously affected members' rights, MCC would have a legal obligation to put the matter to members before action was taken."

Now we have, I said, the blockbuster letter about (members having to pay for entry) the 1999 World Cup from the secretary. "In the light of what has been said, is it valid? Mr president and members of the committee, would you be prepared to tell any member of MCC with a valid member's pass who may be denied entry to Lord's for the World Cup matches that his rights and privileges have not been seriously affected or impaired? (Applause)

"If in front of this audience you are unable to do so, what has happened to your legal obligation to consult us? It was the failure to consult us in 1987 that made passions run so high. There are members here today who are obviously a little unhappy about their club's affairs and believe they should have been consulted. Sir, I think you and the committee are making a big mistake by failing to consult the membership and to take their temperature at regular intervals. You need to take us with you and believe we should have been consulted. The club needs unity and not division. Lord Griffiths once wrote to me and finished his letter with the following words: 'I'm glad we were able to come to an agreement, and it confirms me in my view that most problems arise out of lack of consultation rather than fundamental disagreement.' He was so right.

"If it is not practicable to reconvene the Griffiths working party, another mechanism of similar status must be created as a matter of urgency: the club is not short of talented and influential people. We have the previous prime minister, John Major, amongst us, and I would suggest that perhaps one or two big names from outside the club should be considered – perhaps including a woman for a change. I believe that centre stage should be the two numbered parts of the resolution that have been proposed, but perhaps we could include a third part and ask the working party to think the unthinkable and bring to members some blue-sky ideas to bring our club to the millennium with a secure and exciting future.

"When officers of the club continue to tell me that we must do as we are told (as we were at the sgm of 1966) and not rock the boat for fear of losing the Lord's Tests, the time has come for a long and cool look ahead. (Members: "Hear, hear")

"Mr president, hand to your successor hope and unity and not doubt and division. I respectfully request that you support and recommend the adoption of this resolution." (Applause)

President (Tony Lewis): "Mr Alan Meyer, would you like to add to that?"

Meyer: "I will not take long, because it has all been said either during the meeting or by Nigel Knott. However, I believe the members are now at the top of a steep, slippery slope, down which members' rights and privileges may be further significantly eroded without any prior consultation unless we now get this consultation, which we were promised and guaranteed in 1987 when it last happened." (Applause)

President: "I thank you both for an extremely well conducted and excellently worded resolution. You may both, or certainly one of you, have talked yourself into a job. I will ask the secretary to answer this resolution."

Secretary: "Thank you, president. I know I speak on behalf of all the committee in thoroughly endorsing this resolution. It may sound as though it's rather too late, but there has been for some time the intention to set up a working party. The treasurer, the chairman of finance and I did talk to Nigel Knott and Alan Meyer, and it is clear we need to negotiate, if that is the right word, with the ECB about the matches that belong to the Board. They are their matches and we must have a proper contractual agreement which is acceptable to our club. It is a very difficult situation as I am sure you will appreciate.

Personally, I would like to apologise for not consulting more.

"We have consulted with the members a huge number of times recently, perhaps in your view on the wrong issues rather than on this particular issue. But it is absolutely vital that we take the members with us on this.

"It is very important that your privileges and rights are not eroded. My own view for the World Cup was slightly different, and I do apologise for that. I thought it was different from the normal seasons and the normal Test matches, and I believe that that is what we must address, because the World Cup, although not a unique competition, is a competition that will only come here now every 20 years.

"It is absolutely essential therefore that we talk about the three issues that are bound to come up in any discussion with the Board. The first is the safety issues, which are entirely in MCC's hands: safety and security must be entirely in MCC hands. Secondly, there are the presentational issues, the way in which the game is presented. This brings us into discussion about white or coloured clothing, the kind of advertising and the various things that appear on the replay screen, if indeed a replay screen is in place. That, I think, will take a good deal of discussion, because the ECB's and MCC's views are different.

"The third point, which is clearly the crucial one that really affects members, is the financial or commercial issue. There too, over the years, a number of things have changed, and it is very apparent that they have changed. In some cases they have changed slowly; in other cases they have suddenly been thrust upon us as a member of the Board, and we are a member of the Board, so we are bound by the regulations of the board. But we, as a club, always have an option, and this is the case, I think. with the World Cup. We could have said: 'The terms are unacceptable and we will not have the matches here.'

"It is the committee's responsibility to provide as much first-class and top-class cricket for the members as we possibly can, and on this particular issue it was felt very strongly that the members would not wish the World Cup matches to be played elsewhere. Indeed, it is unthinkable that they would be. The ICC are the owners of the World Cup, and this is the first time that MCC has not been involved with ICC as the secretariat. It has also been passed down to the ECB, which is a new body. which doesn't form part of the Cricket Council of which we were a part. We have one voice on the management Board, but that is all that we have. Therefore, it was the committee's view that there was the little point in coming to the members with a question such as 'Should we say no to the World Cup on these terms?' because the ECB might have been forced to take matches away from Lord's and that would have been very sad.

"The ongoing Test match series, one day internationals and finals are a very different issue that I feel strongly about. It is vital we set up the right working party and I fully support what this resolution says." (Applause)

President: "Does anyone want to make any points on that opinion or can we vote on the resolution?"

Nigel Peters (long-serving committee member): "Simply this, Mr president. I understand that this discussion document and resolution were submitted to the club before the club sent out the Test match and World Cup tickets. In the light of this resolution, it makes it more deplorable that the membership was not consulted or told in advance about the change in membership rights, because clearly Dr Knott and Mr Meyer put the club on notice that there was disquiet and concern about proposals to change our membership rights."

President: "Thank you very much. Can I please have your vote in favour? And those against? Thank you very much. Carried nearly unanimously."

Despite this, there were no repercussions. As with politicians, promises were made – and promises were not kept.

As was to be expected, the resultant staging agreement working party made little progress and I had cause to write to Lord Griffiths again in July 1999.

Dear Lord Griffiths,

I am writing to you in your capacity as the senior MCC statesman in the belief you may be able to assist. As you know I have been concerned for some time over the failure of the MCC committee to honour various pledges made to the MCC members and the secrecy over the financial affairs of the club.

You began to redress matters in 1991 when you answered my wish to have more financial details included in the annual report and accounts and in particular the money paid to the ECB for the use of Lord's. You will remember my main concern centred upon the fact that the club has never been given the proper recognition it deserves for being such a huge benefactor. Immediately following your time as president, messrs Melluish and Hudd removed much of this extra detail and returned to the bad old days of secrecy. My complaints have fallen upon deaf ears.

Since then the committee has responded to my appeal at agm to appoint a new working party under your guidance, to review the failure of the newly created ECB to follow our advice on its constitution. You will recall the importance we attached to the creation of a 'cricket constitution' with the new board of control being made accountable. We remained silent on whether MCC should be part of any new executive. Our offer of assistance in the formulation of a draft 'cricket constitution' has been summarily dismissed.

Kindest regards, Nigel.

Meanwhile I had taken the precaution of asking a question at the 1996 agm of Michael Melluish: "Will members be given the freedom of choice of approving the terms of belonging to the newly constituted ECB?" The president confirmed that ECB accountability was to be a pre-requisite. We were assured of proper consultation and there would be no 'fait accompli.' Soon afterwards and without warning it was announced that MCC would become part of the ECB with the MCC treasurer and secretary included on the board of management. Later, the treasurer joined the ECB World Cup finance committee! It was in 1997 that the ECB issued an ultimatum to MCC to sign a staging agreement that many committee members never saw before it was signed by the secretary. Here was the George Mann/Jack Davies saga all over again. There was no financial consideration in the agreement and no-one of sound mind should ever have accepted the terms.

It is worth remembering that in 1995 the club was asked to build a media centre and new ECB offices for the World Cup. Why were the financial implications of staging the World Cup not discussed and agreed at the same time? Why were members told we could not afford to pay £1.4m to stage the World Cup – was this to be written off as a loss? By charging members it seemed the loss was to be hidden. I raised this further question at the time: "We will be faced with a members' liaison group (Tony Lewis) resulting from the agm fiasco, a staging agreement working party (Charles Fry) and a structure working party (Sir Michael Jenkins) in the belief we can remedy poor governance, a lack of consultation, financial mismanagement and a defective rule book."

The committee expressed a strong disapproval of the president's decision to appoint a members' liaison group, which was wound up prematurely without making a report. In our discussions, important matters were recorded, which included objections to the recommendation of the Jenkins working party that the office of secretary be combined with that of chief executive.

John 'Fingers' Fingleton, long-standing and outspoken MCC member. From a sketch by Martin Mitchell

Charles Rifkind and his family

*From left to right Simon Elliot, Charles Rifkind, Lord Grabiner KC
and Sir Simon Robertson take a break from MCC matters*

"Another unwelcome development."

Chapter 3 – The Wrong People in the Wrong Jobs
A catastrophic commercial enterprise

Chapter 3
The Wrong People in the Wrong Jobs

'Like all dysfunctional systems, it was a mix of a lot of the wrong people in the wrong job, decades of accumulated power, no real scrutiny and insight, a culture of constantly classifying everything to hide mistakes and scrutiny.' (Covid enquiry 2023)

It would be reasonable to assume that any organisation responsible for the laws of cricket and ensuring good governance would apply the basic principles of efficiency and good housekeeping. It is a well-known fact that successful organisations cannot be run by committees, let alone one that depends upon a secretary as chief executive, six assistant secretaries and more than 160 unelected quasi-executive members of various sub-committees advising the main committee, which is responsible for the entire everyday management of everything. MCC, now a Royal Charter Corporation (this came into effect in 2013) with an annual turnover in excess of £55m still stubbornly embraces this extraordinary method of undemocratic government. The consequence has been years of mismanagement, waste and lack of accountability that has had lasting negative results both for the club finances and for the 18,000 full members. This despite in 1984 a special working party's recommendation of a maximum 16,000 MCC members in addition to a maximum of five sub-committees. It also emphasised that there was little or no trading profit. Plus ça change.

The whole purpose of MCC's Royal Charter is to sweep away the time expired disorganised management structure of our private member club to take advantage of the benefits ('presents') endowed by one properly constituted body corporate.

In 1867 MCC's original rule book consisted of four and a half pages. Today this book has spawned more than 50 pages of rules, apparently all approved by members at general meetings, supplemented by a further 70-page book of regulations produced by the committee without member approval. The difference is unclear, destabilising and undemocratic.

No business plans are ever published or acknowledged by the MCC committee. Yet few members seem aware of, or even seem to care about, the damage being caused. Such as it is, this threadbare business model depends largely on the ECB allocating at least two Test matches per year to MCC at Lord's. The MCC- ECB relationship therefore has become fundamental to the club's continued solvency and needs to be as close and cordial as possible. Inevitably, this has resulted in a loss of organisational and commercial independence. Meantime, the committee, which is not remunerated and has incorporated individuals such as Charles Fry who have been prepared to put in countless hours, remains responsible, according to the rules, for the entire management of club affairs. A doctrine of collective responsibility and secrecy ensures that committee members remain unaccountable and immunised from any charges of inefficiency and negligence. The proceedings of all committee meetings are partly enveloped in a shroud of confidentiality. 'Ordinary' members who demand closer scrutiny are considered unwelcome agents provocateurs.

Since MCC members were first alerted to the deficiencies in committee governance and a shocking lack of member communication in 1987 – when the annual meeting broke up in disarray – strenuous efforts have been made to prevent a recurrence.

Logic would dictate a committee solution to redress the obvious weaknesses and improve democratic governance. The exact opposite has occurred with the imposition of draconian measures to strengthen the committee's stranglehold on power. The censorship of member resolutions introduced at sgm's accompanied by committee instructions to vote against anything unpalatable, combined with the further use of remote electronic/postal voting before any agm has been formally convened, complete the sterilisation of member rights and privileges at Lord's. This is governance with a difference with any vestige of democracy being exterminated. Here we have no recognisable corporate structure and an unaccountable executive whereby members are an afterthought.

Ever since the governance of English cricket was thrown into the melting pot by the government in 1968, the game and sport of cricket has been bedevilled by internecine strife between MCC, the TCCB and more recently the ECB. The jewel in the MCC crown has always been Lord's – the generator of very substantial income coveted by the organisers of major matches. Lord's and MCC are synonymous. In a TCCB letter of 1986 the club's secretary, Jack Bailey, was portrayed as the 'baddie' who was preventing the TCCB from doing what they liked at Lord's despite the fact that Bailey was employed by MCC and despite the fact that Lord's is owned by MCC's members. No evidence exists to show what Bailey had done wrong or whether he had acted against the interests of MCC or against the instructions of the club's committee. The departures of Bailey and David Clark, the club's treasurer, which came to light in early 1987, were the culmination of years of steadily increasing pressure from the TCCB executive, an organisation seeking to increase its authority over matches played at Lord's and its share of the extremely attractive facilities available to MCC members. Clark wrote to the TCCB chairman supporting Jack and the MCC secretariat. That had the effect of bringing him into the line of fire as well.

It was said the secretary of MCC was too powerful and he had not consulted the committee, yet Jack had warned the committee of the way things were going. He had said all along there was a danger of a takeover and he has been proved correct, time and time again. The committee insisted that he must make no public statements about what had occurred.

Alan Meyer, the club's solicitor, referred to the severe problems faced by George Mann and Doug Insole, two of the foremost names and administrators in English cricket, in the context of divided loyalties and the problems faced by MCC as a result. Meyer was in a very awkward position as he knew the affairs of the club inside out and had been responsible for giving advice on all manner of topics; he had acted for the club for decades. The rules and the rules of the International Cricket Council had all come within his domain, as had the Kerry Packer World Series Cricket hearing following the breakaway of many of the leading players in the world, seeking greater remuneration, in 1977.

Meyer had sought the advice of leading counsel regarding the whole TCCB/MCC affair, advice which had been passed on to the committee. Now the club lawyers were in no man's land. Having given and sought opinions on the proper procedure for the annual general meeting of 1987, they found that matters had gone beyond a point where, in all conscience, they could support the committee in the line it was taking. It was courageous on their part to stand by their guns and in the end they were to pay dearly for it. It was not difficult to predict an instant and angry reaction and Bailey's analysis of the stormy bicentennial agm three days later is worth recording.

Before and after the annual general meeting (which he did not attend) Bailey entertained a number of friends at his house. John Woodcock of *The Times* remarked to the former club solicitor how sad it was that so many of the 'dissidents' used the secretary's home as a base; as though some enemy camp had been set up. Bailey had known most of the guests for ages   all of them, except Clark and two recent members of the committee, Fred Millett and Colin Smith, ordinary members of the club. All called to express their condolences, genuinely concerned, as friends are liable to be, over the turn affairs had taken. I was one of those present and flourished a copy of the working party report of 1984.

"How do l get the president to answer various questions I want to put?" I asked Bailey. "It's very difficult," he acknowledged. "But I believe that the chairman would be hard put not to ask you to speak if you raised a point of order."

That was the extent of the conversation on the subject of the annual general meeting of 1987, the extent of the 'gathering of dissidents' mentioned by Woodcock of *The Times*. The outcome of that agm has been mentioned earlier: for the first time in the club's 200 year-old history the report and accounts were not adopted. A member, Robin Bourne, summed up the meeting in a letter to the press which contained the following passages: "The vote …was overwhelming. So much so, the president (Colin Cowdrey) incredulous and confused, put the motion to adopt a second time. The result of this ill-advised move was, if anything, even more overwhelming. In view of the reported remarks of the acting club secretary that it was not a vote of no confidence, it is only fair to members who were not able to be present to inform them that the vote came as close to being one of no confidence as was possible without making such a motion specifically. The fact is that the meeting was chaotic from start to finish and was a demonstration of the committee's incompetence. Accommodation was totally inadequate – large numbers of members couldn't get in and it was fortunate the vote was clear cut.

"…Even now we are not clearly informed of the safeguards that are supposed to have been agreed with TCCB for members' rights and privileges. However, it did become clear that Jack Bailey had consistently stood for the best interests of MCC members and that gradually the committee was conceding more and more to the demands of the TCCB. There was no doubt that the members were right behind him on that."

The letter went on to criticise the fact that the TCCB had been guaranteed £225,000 from the proceeds of MCC's bicentenary match and that they could only hold the fixture on their own ground with the consent of the TCCB. And continued: "The way forward is for the (annual) report to be amended so that the club's lawyers can endorse it and for the agm to be reconvened. Yesterday, it was adjourned before the business of the meeting was completed. There should be no question of trying to push through the report as it stands by the device of a postal vote…. running the club behind closed doors with little reference to the membership should come to an end. That was what yesterday's meeting was about."

The contents of the story, resembling something from a novel, left me dumfounded. It was an extraordinary situation in which the secretary of MCC had been removed from office, the treasurer had resigned, and the lawyer was rumoured to have refused to endorse the bicentenary report and accounts. This was serious stuff.

What transpired four days later was that Cowdrey had had secret talks with the TCCB chairman, Raman Subba Row, on the use of Lord's in the absence of any contractual staging agreement being approved by MCC members, the owners of Lord's. The pandemonium that ensued at the agm was in itself enough to fire my innate hatred of secrecy and injustice. This was naked dictatorship in action, even supported by Sir Oliver Popplewell, who was then a trustee, in his effort to defend the indefensible action of the MCC committee. He was swamped by a tidal wave of member opposition and an adjournment.

The Times cricket correspondent (Woodcock) was a great friend of Cowdrey. Like so many commentators, within the game though detached from it, he could see the wood for the trees, but were they the right wood and the right trees?

"To take the heat out of Wednesday's meeting," he wrote, "all that was needed could have been a clear statement of the terms of the TCCB's rights (they have been much the same for the last eight years) together with reassurances that MCC's patrimony was being forcefully and strictly protected and would never be further compromised without being put to the vote."

But was that really the case?

For one thing the MCC committee had clearly been forced to give the TCCB, as a result of the previous 12 months, rights far beyond anything previously contemplated. For another, MCC's 'patrimony' was *not* being forcefully and strictly protected. The main hope was that it might be now that the members were aware of what had been going on.

Following the adjourned agm, I and nine other playing members contributed £500 each towards a fighting fund. We were advised by the law firm Frere Cholmeley. In the meantime Alan Meyer had been sacked for telling the truth – an egregious example of an abuse of committee power. Our counsel's opinion made it very clear that the agm agenda remained undetermined and a re-convened agm was required to complete the ordinary business with the members present being required by law to approve the items through the traditional voting of those being present. This agenda included the approval of trustees and the formality of announcing a new president. All attempts to ensure a re-convened agm was held were rebuffed and so was the inclusion of an sgm requisition supported by 220 signatories with an offer to share the expenses. These were dark days for MCC.

However, following this agm disaster the committee decided to take legal advice that resulted in the following expensive document being drafted by two leading counsels:

MCC
The case for full disclosure

1. The MCC annual report, paragraph 3, page 9 states as follows:

    'In the interests of the members, and with the

necessary safeguards to their rights, the committee has affirmed the Test and County Cricket Board's ultimate responsibility for major matches played at Lord's under its jurisdiction. In its turn the Board acknowledges the key role that MCC continues to play, not only at Lord's, but nationally and internationally also.'

2. What is NOT in issue is the TCCB's overall and ultimate responsibility for major matches at Lord's, or elsewhere. That has been the TCCB.'s responsibility since 1968 when MCC created the Board, and does not need to be affirmed again. However, what IS IN issue is whether MCC's committee, under pressure from the TCCB, may now have conceded to the TCCB 'overall and ultimate authority and control' over possibly everything at such major matches at Lord's without, either, consulting or notifying the MCC members, and perhaps without adequate safeguards.

3. At the agm the club's then solicitors, Messrs. Halsey Lightly & Hemsley, made it clear through their partner responsible for MCC's affairs, Alan Meyer, that the club had been advised on April 21 1987 in writing that the above quoted paragraph of the annual report was not correct. In addition, in the same letter the club had been advised that it was necessary to advise the members with regard to the two nominations by the committee for trustee and that the members should have been advised, to comply with Rule 26, that Mr George Mann would have attained the age of 70 at the time of his proposed re-appointment. Further, the club was advised that the members should have been told of the potential conflict of interest of both nominees as former chairmen of the TCCB with their continuing roles in TCCB and given an explanation why the committee considered that the members could safely ignore such potential conflicts of interest.

4. Following the annual general meeting on May 6 1987 the committee of the club notified the club's lawyers that their appointment as solicitors to the club had been terminated by the committee with immediate effect.
5. The advice given to the committee on April 21 1986 and in subsequent correspondence and attendance at a committee meeting immediately before the agm on May 6 1987 was based on a detailed knowledge of the facts relating to the negotiations between MCC and the TCCB which began in July 1983 and largely ended in October 1986. It was also based on the advice obtained from leading counsel on at least three occasions relating to MCC's position in connection with the negotiations with the Board.

The committee did not affirm the Board's ultimate responsibility for major matches at Lord's. Such an offer was made to the Board by letter dated June 30 1986, but that offer was rejected by the Board on July 2 1986.

Subsequently, by a letter dated July 28 1986, the committee affirmed 'the overall and ultimate responsibility of the Board' coupled with assurances that MCC's committee had obtained from its secretariat a clear undertaking of full co-operation with the Board and its staff. In that letter there was a reservation in favour of MCC reserving the right of MCC to put matters to its members "if the Board's responsibilities were exercised in a way that seriously affected members' rights." Previously, in MCC's letter dated June 30 1986, MCC had attempted to ensure, firstly, that the Board would not seek to regulate the rights of MCC's members at Lord's, and secondly that it would not be proper for the Board to direct MCC employees in any way as to the manner in which they carried out such duties and responsibilities. The Board, in its reply, stated that what it required was "a one paragraph letter acknowledging the Board's overall authority over the matches played at Lord's, and confirming that MCC committee had received an unambiguous assurance of co-operation from the MCC secretary and his secretariat.

Eventually, by a letter dated September 17 1986, the chairman of the Board stated, after an earlier unhappy exchange of letters, "However, I believe that when the executive meets on October 5 it will want to give a new relationship, based on your guidelines, a fair trial … In the meantime, it would be helpful to see a copy of your proposed guidelines."

The former president of MCC, Mr. J.G.W. Davies, who had conducted the negotiations with the Board on MCC's behalf, backed up by the committee at its regular meetings, prepared draft guidelines for MCC's secretary and secretariat which stated 'inter alia' on page 1:

'It must be recognised that in respect of staging major matches at Lord's the committee has yielded some degree of sovereignty to the Board. The Board have declared that they hope to settle matters bearing on matches by agreement with MCC: but where this is not possible, their instructions must be accepted. Certain exceptions to this principle are mentioned below and should be recognised by the TCCB. But in general you may have to accommodate changes to which in the past you would have advocated resistance.

'The committee see the latest developments, unwelcome as they may be as a restriction on MCC's autonomy, as an opportunity for constructive action …'

The former solicitors of the club were instructed by the treasurer and secretary to obtain an opinion of leading counsel relating to MCC's situation at that juncture – May 1986 – in connection with the negotiations with the TCCB and the developments which had occurred within such negotiations. That opinion, which eventually was a Joint opinion of Mr. Thomas Morison QC and Mr. Patrick Milmo QC was dated June 23 1986 and stated in its conclusion section 9 as follows:-

'AT PRESENT, THE TCCB ARE ASKING FOR A COMMITMENT BY MCC TO THE PRINCIPLE OF OVERALL BOARD AUTHORITY. FOR UNDERSTANDABLE REASONS, MCC ARE SEEKING CLARIFICATION OF THE EXTENT AND MEANING OF SUCH COMMITMENT. IN OUR OPINION THE MCC COMMITTEE SHOULD CONTINUE TO PURSUE THEIR NEGOTIATIONS WITH THE TCCB AND ASCERTAIN PRECISELY WHERE THE STICKING POINTS ARE. THE MEMBERSHIP SHOULD THEN BE PRESENTED WITH A PACKAGE, WITH OR WITHOUT RECOMMENDATION FOR ACCEPTANCE BY THE MCC COMMITTEE, SETTING OUT THE BEST DEAL WHICH THE COMMITTEE CAN ACHIEVE THROUGH NEGOTIATION. IT IS FOR THE MEMBERS TO DECIDE WHETHER TO ACCEPT SUCH A PACKAGE. WE TAKE THIS VIEW NOT JUST BECAUSE SUCH A PROCESS SEEMS TO US TO FOLLOW FROM THE (FINAL WORKING PARTY) REPORT AND ITS ACCEPTANCE BY THE MEMBERS, BUT ALSO FOR TWO FURTHER REASONS:

1. THE M.C.C. IS A PRIVATE MEMBERS' CLUB AND THE MEMBERS HAVE A RIGHT NOT TO HAVE THEIR RIGHTS ADVERSELY AFFECTED WITHOUT THEIR CONSENT, IN THE ABSENCE OF SOME EXPRESS DELEGATION BY THEM TO THE COMMITTEE.
2. THE POTENTIAL CONFLICT OF INTEREST

ARISES BETWEEN THE TCCB AND MCC COMMITTEE AND WE REFER TO MR. MORISON'S OPINION ON THIS TOPIC DATED JULY 4 1984."

1. Accordingly, it would appear that, as stated by the two leading counsel, the committee had absolutely no power to grant such affirmations to the Board, which in the light of the guidelines, constituted an affirmation of "OVERALL AND ULTIMATE AUTHORITY AND CONTROL" of possibly all detail relating to major matches played at Lord's under the Board's jurisdiction. Of the matches played at Lord's each year, probably only the Eton v Harrow match does not fall within the description 'major matches.'
2. There was of course absolutely no need to give any assurances at all about the Board's overall and ultimate responsibility because that has been enshrined in the Board's constitution since its establishment by MCC in 1968.
3. It would seem, in the absence of full information and disclosure, that the committee may, (i) have exceeded their powers, (ii) not told the members the truth about what has been granted, and (iii) totally failed to obtain any adequate cricketing, or other, safeguards from the Board at the time of the annual report and the subsequent annual general meeting on May 6 1987.

'In addition, in parallel with the negotiations on this matter, there were negotiations both with regard to MCC's future share of the Test match pool, along with that of other Test match grounds, and also the compensation to be paid by MCC to the Board for being permitted to stage the bicentennial match at Lord's in August 1987. These financial negotiations have resulted in MCC members being required to lose considerable sums of money. It would seem that a combination of the financial losses at the Board's requirement, coupled with the loss of autonomy at Lord's as a result of the Board pressure, conflict enormously with the nonsense of the statement in the annual report to the effect 'the Board acknowledges the key role that MCC continues to play.' Certainly MCC, as a major source of revenue to the Test match pool, has a key role in the finances of the pool, and also a continuing key role in the playing of cricket both nationally and internationally. As Sir Donald Bradman stated in his bicentennial article, to someone from abroad it is quite something to be able to return to his country and to say "I've been to Lord's." In cricketing terms, of course, Lord's is the mecca of all cricketers and the peak of their ambitions, which are to play in a Test match at Lord's, and better, to make 50 runs or 100 runs, or to take five wickets in a Test at Lord's. This is a cricketing fact which must remain a vital and key one in the world of cricket.

'Accordingly, the members are entitled to a full disclosure and to be told about the safeguards which have been built in, if any, and why control of many cricketing and other facets at Lord's now have been given up to the TCCB without notifying the members. The committee must explain why they have taken this course of action when the interim report of the working party made it clear that control of Lord's must never be given up, and the final working party report adopted by the members at the May 1984 agm made it clear that the committee were for the future to enter into commercial negotiations with regard to the playing of cricket at Lord's.

'The committee must explain why immediately following the assumption of the office of president, Mr Colin Cowdrey took every step to ensure that Mr Bailey was sacked. Further, why Mr Cowdrey as a current chairman of a TCCB committee has not declared his interest. Further, why in the committee's nominations for trustees of the club they found it necessary to nominate two members of the committee who had enormously strong TCCB connections when it would be a very easy matter to find two reputable members of the club to act as its trustees with no potential or other conflict of interest situation at all.

'The committee must explain why the treasurer of the club felt it necessary to resign in December 1986, and perhaps why such a decision was not announced to the public and members until notifying the members of the 'early retirement' of the secretary in January 1987.

'Perhaps the committee should explain why, in conjunction with these two departures it then became necessary to dismiss the club's long-serving solicitors without reason on May 22 1987 after the club's solicitors had been forced to point out on April 21 1987 that the annual report, and particularly paragraph 3 on page 9 were incorrect, and therefore not capable of being put to the members in that form. The mistake was not the solicitors' mistake. The mistake was due to the incompetence of the officers and the committee in putting out an incorrect report.

'As can be seen clearly from the extracts from the correspondence between MCC and the Board from June to September 1986, the committee in the annual report did not provide proper disclosure, or any disclosure at all, of exactly what had been conceded to the Board. Furthermore, the committee explained in no way why it had been necessary to concede now additional rights to the Board at Lord's over and above the rights they had had since 1968 at Lord's and all other Test match grounds where the Board delegate to the ground authority the staging of major matches. (9.6.87)

'The committee decided to ignore lawful protocol and called their own sgm on July 30 1987 at Central Hall Westminster to seek what amounted to a vote of confidence in the president (Cowdrey) and the MCC committee. A committee defeat was out of the question with 95 per cent of the membership being encouraged to stay at home and exercise a postal vote for the committee before the sgm had even been convened! The committee case was placed before the members at sgm audience by an emotional committee member. Furthermore it was maintained the green paper (1984) was a document of substance; having been issued to the membership and having been approved, the membership had every right to expect it to be followed in every detail.'

Lord David Pannick says "Don't Panic!"

> **MARYLEBONE CRICKET CLUB**
>
> 200th ANNIVERSARY
>
> # ANNUAL REPORT - 1987
>
> ### ANNUAL GENERAL MEETING
>
> Notice is hereby given that the Annual General Meeting will be held in the Lord's Banqueting and Conference Centre on WEDNESDAY, 6th MAY, 1987 at 2.30 p.m.
> The President, Mr. M. C. Cowdrey, will take the Chair.
>
> *To be followed immediately by a*
>
> SPECIAL GENERAL MEETING
>
> Called in accordance with Rule 49 of the Rules of the Club to approve amendments to the 1980 Code of the Laws of Cricket.
>
> ### OUTLINE OF PROCEDURE
>
> 1. The Report and Accounts
> 2. Questions arising from the Report and Accounts
> 3. The adoption of the Report and Accounts
> 4. Resolution for discussion proposed by a Member in accordance with Rule 42
> 5. Any other business
> 6. Nomination by the President of his successor
> 7. Special General Meeting

This 200th Annual Report was the first in the Cub's history to be rejected

Chapter 4 – Meetings and Machinations
The trashing of Member Rights and Privileges

Chapter 4
Meetings and Machinations

The day of the July 1987 MCC sgm at Central Hall, Westminster, arrived, the meeting convened following the accounts having not been accepted at the agm in May, and a committee stooge by the name of Michael Sissons, was appointed to open the batting. He was noted for telling members that they should be grateful for committee members, such as himself, giving of their time without charge.

"David Clark implies that the club's solicitors were dismissed for conveying unpalatable truths. I am sorry to have to deal with this question tonight, but I think it is required of us. This is not so. The evident support by the senior partner of Halsey, Lightly & Hemsley for the Bailey-Clark view led the committee reluctantly to conclude that the strength of his personal feelings was clouding his judgment. No fair-minded person who was at this year's agm could have expected us to allow the president or, as it turns out, the treasurer, to chair this meeting today without the benefit of detached, professional legal opinion from a different source.

"An elected committee is always fair game, and rightly so. Nobody pretends that we couldn't have made a better job of communicating all this to you earlier this year. That is acknowledged, and I hope the past tradition that the inner cabal of MCC behaved as some sort of secret society has gone out of the window for ever and that never again will members feel that they have been excluded from matters of substance at Lord's.

May I at the same time ask you to consider that this committee is far more broadly based than it ever has been before. Its opinions are formed by a mixture of cricket experience on the one hand and business, professional and public affairs experience on the other 13, which I suggest is about right. I have been grateful to serve on it and I hope that many other ordinary members will have the chance to do so. <u>I may say that it is damned hard work.</u> Most of us have brought professional skills to the service of the club. For example, David Male and Sir Anthony Tuke and their colleagues on the estates and finance committees have put enormous time, hard work and expertise into the planning, construction and selling of the Mound Stand and into a root-and-branch programme for the refurbishment of the ground which leaves no part of it unconsidered. If they had charged for their services at a remotely commercial rate, the club would be facing bills of many thousands of pounds.

We have done a lot in these years of which we can be proud. I think it is valid, not that it does much good now, to point the finger at past committees from around 1974 onwards for allowing the problem between the TCCB and the secretary, which became as much a problem of personalities as of policies, to grow a cancer at the heart of this club.

'As between the committee and the secretary it became an open question as to who was master and who was servant. It is to Colin Cowdrey's credit that, with the overwhelming support of this year's committee, he has finally grasped the nettle. Future presidents and committees will thank him for doing so. The presidency had become a bed of nails. Finally, there are no heroes and there are no villains in this, only casualties, and I hope no one will persuade you otherwise. When a hundred years from now Tony Lewis's successor writes the history of 300 years of MCC he, or maybe she, will surely conclude that this has been a particularly difficult period in the evolution of the club. I am equally certain that Jack Bailey and David Clark will be seen as devoted members of the club who played substantial and constructive parts in that evolution, for all that has happened this year. That irony is our tragedy and theirs. I suggest that enough blood has been spilt. Let us use this afternoon to make peace and to move forward. Most important, let us behave in such a way that that future historians will have something good to say about all of us. Thank you."

The scene was set for me to take the new ball and open the bowling for the opposition:

"Mr chairman, my lords, gentlemen. We have been advised by solicitors and counsel. I would like to thank you for making special arrangements to allow us to present our case to this meeting tonight. At the outset I wish to add to your good wishes and to express my own personal sorrow over our president's illness, and I wish him a speedy recovery. I am slightly disappointed that you (Hubert Doggart) are sitting in the chair tonight as treasurer. (I believed Sir Anthony Tuke, as chairman of finance, should have been in charge of proceedings). It is a slightly controversial appointment, and I would have preferred that you had sat there as a member chosen by the committee under Rule 44, because you will obviously be aware that your appointment had to be ratified in the annual report that was rejected.

"I am going to divide my presentation into three parts – firstly, concerning points of order; secondly, concerning our efforts to ensure that views other than those of the committee were circulated with the postal ballot in an attempt to achieve a balance of opinion; and, thirdly, our reaction to the committee document of July 8. John Pretlove will be summing up for us and will be providing some constructive advice at the end of the proceedings.

Let me emphasise that this sgm has been of the committee's own making because of their failure to respond to their legal advice and to inform members fully on matters of fundamental principle in the annual report. There are a number of questions that I shall raise, Mr chairman, which the members will want answered this evening.

"Please let me underline from the start that we deplore the personalisation of this issue and we consider the proceedings to be concerned with the relationship of the committee with MCC membership. The role of the TCCB in professional cricket is not in dispute. What has been a matter of great concern and remains so is who runs Lord's, why does the committee ignore the working party report which was commissioned by the committee and adopted at the agm in 1984, why have we lost half our officers and the club's solicitors in one year? Issues of fundamental principle are at stake and the concerted attempts by the committee to trivialise matters shows a grave lack of understanding.

"There is ample evidence to suggest that the manner in which this sgm has been organised and the circumstances in which the postal ballot is being conducted are one-sided, biased, unreasonable and probably unlawful. I wish to concentrate initially on extremely narrow issues of fundamental principle which will call into question the proceedings outlined in the committee document of July 8. In our view the committee should be reconvening the agm, and the revised report and accounts should form an integral part of this document.

"Following the overwhelming rejection on two occasions of the annual report and accounts in their entirety, it would seem logical to inform those members not present at the agm about the substance of the case against the committee's report and accounts. My own attempts to ensure that this was done have been steadfastly opposed, despite the fact that I informed the president by letter dated May 9 that 180 signatures would be obtained if necessary to ensure that all the necessary information was circulated if a postal vote was to take place. Our group has made strenuous efforts, with legal backing, to ensure that additional information could be made available to members, but these have been frustrated by the committee. Those of you present at the meeting today should be aware that the resolution on the postal voting form and on the back page of the committee document is incorrect and highly misleading. I have a letter here from the club's new solicitors, Simmons & Simmons, which states: 'The appointment of the two trustees was dealt with and voted upon separately [at the agm] and they stand despite the fact that the report and accounts were not adopted.' This is untrue. They state earlier in the same letter:

'The matter was not put to a formal vote.'

"The report and accounts that were rejected as a whole at the agm on two occasions are, therefore, no longer being reconsidered by the committee in their entirety, despite the complete absence of any statement to the contrary. Furthermore, despite what Simmons & Simmons have said in their letter, they totally contradict their opinion that the trustee appointments can be considered separately by stating later in the same letter: 'It is invariable in any club or company meeting to ask for the adoption of the report and accounts as a whole.'

"There seems to be, Mr chairman, some considerable confusion in the opinion of our new solicitors. Let me say that, whatever Simmons & Simmons say in their letter, no vote was taken at the agm. The then solicitors, Halsey, Lightly & Hemsley, represented by Mr Alan Meyer, informed us that they had written to the committee on April 21 to say that it was necessary for the report to be valid to inform members that under rule 26 Mr Mann would be over 70 years of age on his appointment and, in addition, to explain why the committee felt that it was safe to ignore the potential conflicts of interest which were obvious in the cases of both Mr Mann and Mr Insole. The president informed only those present at the agm that he felt there was sufficient reason to override the age requirement under rule 26 in the case of Mr Mann, but he failed to mention any conflict of interest that inevitably arises. The agm business agenda was clearly and unequivocally stated on the front page of the annual report and following the questions at item 2, formal adoption was required at item 3.

"Those present at the agm will remember that I tried to raise a point of order early on in the meeting and the president stated that he wished to deal with it at the end. Amongst other things, which included an objection to the wording in paragraph 3 at page 9 by the club solicitor, I wished to raise the question about conflict of interest where the trustees were concerned. By making me wait until the end of the questioning, the president was in effect confirming that the report and accounts were being considered as a whole rather than in part. I submit, Mr chairman, that the trustees' appointments are invalid and remain so whatever the result of this vote today, because there has still been no disclosure to the membership as a whole about the age limitation in the case of Mr Mann being over 70 years and the conflict of interest in the cases of both Mr Mann and Mr Insole.

"This committee has already failed twice to receive the necessary support for the adoption of their report and accounts at agm and I am now suggesting that this same committee has moved even further from the principles of democracy and justice by their latest efforts in what is fast becoming a Grace Gates scandal (laughter). One must ask the question: why is the committee going to these extraordinary lengths to prevent a fair and **impartial** debate on these weighty issues? Have you really something to hide? We have a quite extraordinary situation. We have in effect two juries who are being asked to give their verdict on two separate resolutions. On the one hand a great jury of perhaps 16,500 members is being given carefully selected evidence prepared by the committee, expressing the view that everything in the garden is lovely and supported by a personal letter from the president appealing for loyalty. Without any evidence to the contrary, is it not as plain as a pikestaff how this jury will vote? On the other hand, we have a lesser jury here today, who have an opportunity to hear views other than those of the committee and facts which suggest that something is rotten in the state of Denmark. They will be able to form a balanced view after the various arguments have been heard today and vote accordingly. They will be better informed and their verdict is bound to be of greater validity than the one of the great absent jury. But I am afraid the committee has decreed that under rule 37 this is not the case. They are in effect saying that with their powers of complete discretion, they are able to stand reason on its head and they are above the law.

"Mr chairman, the members of this great club really do deserve better treatment. We are not idiots and I think that you should realise that we are extraordinarily unhappy and disturbed by these events. You must also accept that your committee may not enjoy our confidence in the way that you are conducting our affairs, and I cannot see how we can be expected to continue acting in this manner.

"I must emphasise that these are not just my personal views. Our group has taken advice from solicitors and counsel and it is the considered opinion of both that the committee has acted unlawfully in failing to consult the membership on a number of contentious issues of constitutional importance. It is their considered view that there exist ample grounds for legal action against you and the committee on the way that this ballot is being conducted. I hope, Mr chairman, that you will allow Mr Alan Meyer to speak in his capacity as the club's former solicitor. I believe that he will be able to make an important contribution on these legal matters. I am certain that the members here tonight will wish to hear him speak. (Members: "Hear, hear")

"I will now move on to our efforts to have our views heard. The committee was informed in plenty of time that if a postal vote was to take place we would wish to have our own material circulated, and this was prepared in readiness by June 25. In addition, we indicated our willingness to contribute towards the extra costs, if thought appropriate, and we supported our request with 200 signatures delivered to the secretary on July 7, in accordance with rule 43. We did this to avoid the extra cost and inconvenience of a further sgm in order to have our views circulated with those of the committee on this occasion. We cannot understand why this reasonable request has been refused and offer this as further evidence of serious shortcomings and the questionable value and morality of this meeting tonight.

"Simmons & Simmons state in their letter that there is no reason why those holding views opposed to the committee should consider that they have a right to be heard 'in the case of an sgm called by the committee themselves, and where there is a postal ballot.'

"The point here is that under rule 43 we have collected the requisite number of signatures for us to have our case heard by all the members and not just those here today. We were responsible by reasoned argument for the rejection of the report and accounts at the agm. Mr chairman, these tactics are more familiar in Russia than in our democracy. The great club deserves much better standards of behaviour.

"Let us now look at the document itself. I would start by drawing your attention, again, to the letter from Simmons & Simmons, who state:

'The committee is unanimous in believing that its present policy in relation to the TCCB is the correct one and indeed, almost certainly, the only sensible one. Well, Mr chairman, this is a rather arrogant statement. It is a classic case of 'I am Sir Oracle, and when I open my lips let no dog bark!' How can you be so certain? Do you have a monopoly of wisdom and knowledge on the committee?

"Perhaps you could turn to page 4 of the sgm document 'Working Party Report.' The reason for this report was the rumblings of discontent among the membership. You have stated that you believe that you have a degree of discretion. NO! This is a legally binding report which limits the committee's powers. It was accepted by the committee, which pledged that it should be implemented. Reference is made to 'The 1983 Paper' – what is this document, where is it, what are we talking about? It was interesting to hear Mr Sissons refer to overall and ultimate authority at Lord's, but in your document you refer to the overall and ultimate responsibility, and I understand that this has been the cause of a considerable amount of what the Judge (Popplewell) referred to at the agm as hours and hours of sterile argument. The committee cannot give away overall authority at Lord's under rule 37 without first going to the membership for their approval. Under 'Further negotiation' the document states in heavy type:

'The committee ... believed that one of its major duties to members of MCC was to ensure the preservation of the full programme at Lord's.'

"I hope, Mr chairman, you will permit me to run on just a little bit longer and will not ping your egg timer, because this is a matter of extreme importance. I apologise for taking a little bit of extra time and I will do my best to finish quickly. 'Secretary and treasurer' on page 6, and the guidelines. Who prepared these guidelines? Where are they? Are they confidential, and if so why? The first sentence of the 'summary' is contradictory; it is nonsensical. At the top of page 7 the documents states:

'Members should also note the following points: assurances had been given to the TCCB ... the committee has been advised that the assurances are not enforceable in a court of law.... the giving of assurances makes no difference to the real situation.'

"Mr chairman, really. It is rather deceitful, isn't it, to give assurances that are not enforceable in a court of law? The committee of MCC should act with integrity and probity. Rover tickets under 'members' rights' – you talk about 'one minor respect.' A £3 a head payment to the TCCB as opposed to perhaps £100 for a ticket – yes, it might be minor, but this is a fundamental point of principle. MCC objected in principle to members paying at any time for admission to their ground at Lord's, but now apparently they think it wrong to revoke its acceptance of the TCCB's decision to raise member admission charges.

"We move on to page 8 and counsel's opinions. You may remember, Mr chairman, that in a personal meeting I had with you I asked you and the president whether these counsel's opinions had been sought by Mr Clark and Mr Bailey off their own bat without the consent of the committee and you did not in fact say anything to the contrary. In fact you led me to believe that these opinions were sought with the knowledge of at least the president and possibly other members of the committee. So it is wholly wrong to give the impression that these opinions were sought as a personal opinion. It is disgraceful. It is a travesty of the truth. Counsel has declared that 'members' consent was required before their rights were adversely affected".' They have been – what proposal from the TCCB was counsel considering? Why is a proposal required?

"I will finish very shortly, Mr chairman. The Touche Ross report states that £100,000 more will be going from members' funds this next year. The financial arrangements – there is no mention of the TCCB levy on the club, and perhaps Sir Anthony Tuke could explain his inaccurate answer to my question at the agm and furthermore clarify his rather muddled statement about the match receipts from the TCCB in 1985 and 1986.

"I will conclude. If you move on to page 11, the conclusions of the committee, again just as an example of the imbalance:

'To vote in favour of the committee an 'X' should be placed in the 'For' column of the postal voting form.'

"Well, Mr chairman, what about those who might want to vote against? (Applause) In my opinion this is a disgraceful abuse of committee power. It is 'The seeming truth which cunning times put on to entrap the wisest.'

"I end by repeating the questions that I asked at the beginning. Who runs Lord's? Why does the committee ignore this working party report, which was commissioned by the committee and adopted at the agm in 1984? Why have we lost half the officers of the club and club's solicitors in one year? Mr chairman, these issues will not go away and they cannot be swept under the carpet. Thank you." (Applause)

The chairman (Hubert Doggart): "Thank you, Dr Knott, for

your contribution to this discussion. I want to open it to the meeting, but I think it right that one or two of the points at least that Dr Knott made should be answered. I think I counted 15 or 16 questions. If I could just make three points from the chair – one affects me, so I think it fair that it should be answered – I shall then turn for the financial matters to Sir Anthony Tuke, our chairman of finance, and for the more general matters to Mr Jack Davies, a past president of MCC and very much involved in things in 1986.

"The three points I am going to make are quite simple. First, I would say that the committee have nothing to hide, that there isn't anything rotten in the state of Denmark, as Dr Knott claims, that the committee does not claim a monopoly of wisdom. It very much hopes, first, that members will think that it is a fair and full memorandum – I know Dr Knott does not – and, secondly, that this will be a full, fair and open discussion.

"The second point I would like to make concerns the report and the accounts and the references to the trustees and myself. Of course the report and accounts were not adopted at the agm, otherwise we would not be here."

To this very day the 1987 bicentenary agm report and accounts remain unapproved and the ordinary business agenda outstanding. Unsurprisingly the postal vote was introduced at the sgm to carry the day with absent members providing more than 90 per cent of the votes. The committee retired to the pavilion thinking it had extinguished the member rebellion whilst in truth it was the beginning of a long drawn-out battle in the form of an ongoing war with the gradual obliteration of member rights and privileges at Lord's the result. The trustees remained mute at the time, and have done so on many occasions since and as a result have had their duties and responsibilities whittled into oblivion.

"Silicon Valley tech billionaires running cricket - what can possibly go wrong?"

Chapter 5 – The ECB – A Cuckoo in the Lord's Nest
The phantom 30,000 MCC Shares in a Captive Insurance Company in Guernsey

Chapter 5
The ECB –
A Cuckoo in the Lord's Nest

In 1987 the TCCB's offices at Lord's, an unappealing edifice at the Nursery End, cost £400,000 to construct. The governing body was granted a 25-year lease at a heavily discounted rental. Before the expiry, I wrote to the secretary and chief executive of MCC to enquire about the new terms to ensure no discount was included and that a full London price would be charged in future. He declined to provide any detail. We are reminded at regular intervals by the ECB of the ever-present threat of having major matches played elsewhere if we, MCC, fail to toe the party line at Lord's. Nobody raised an eyebrow when the list of Test match grounds was expanded to include Durham, Cardiff and Hampshire so as to enable the ECB to dilute the value of the Lord's equity even further.

I have lost count of being warned by MCC's secretary not to rock the boat as we have established "a very good working relationship with the ECB." A relationship of fawning sycophancy more like it. If Lord's cannot survive from cricket income alone, the obvious answer is supplementary rental and commercial income. The implications of the commercial attractions of The Hundred pose a serious threat to the future of Lord's. It was never Sir George 'Gubby' Allen's wish for the ground to become a floodlit stadium or an arena in which the activities include the use of various coloured cricket balls becoming a monetised threat.

In 1993 some bright spark in the accounts department of TCCB decided to research a cost-saving exercise on the insurance premiums paid to cover ticket losses as a result of bad weather. A decision was made to create a captive insurance company offshore in Guernsey to be named, for some unknown reason, Reigndei. Charles Fry, an MCC individual through and through who had founded his own insurance firm, Johnson Fry, explained this company was to be known as 'Rainy Day' specialising in 'pluvial insurance.'

A total of 595,000 £1 shares were to be issued partly paid (95p) to the 18 first-class counties, MCC and the Minor Counties Cricket Association, held in trust by Derbeyork Trustee Company Ltd. (DBY). It was created as part of the mechanism to provide insurance payments for the lost income on big match days.

> *The necessary DBY extraordinary general meeting was held on June 24 1993: To undertake, perform and execute any trust or discretion and the distribution amongst the beneficiaries or other persons entitled to it, of any income or capital and whether in money or specie in furtherance of any discretion obligation or permission: for the above purposes to hold, deal with, manage, direct the management of buy, sell, exchange, mortgage, charge, lease, dispose of, or grant any right or interest in, over or upon any real or personal property of any kind, including contingent and reversionary interests in any property and to undertake and carry on any business, undertaking or transaction in the matters and for the purposes aforesaid to act solely or jointly with any other corporation or body.*

Brian Havill (ECB) was secretary and director of DBY for 11 years from 2004 to 2015 and also the director of Reigndei

Ltd. He was in a position of complete control as financial director of the ECB concerning the insurance transactions involving Reigndei. Three directors, messrs F Chamberlain (chairman TCCB), MP Murray and AC Smith (TCCB directors), were made responsible for the governance and administration. The share capital was set at 100 x £1 shares and three were issued to Murray, Dennis Silk and Smith.

The disclosure statement published on December 31 2001 read: 'Derbeyork Ltd is the legal owner of 100 per cent of the ordinary share capital of Reigndei Ltd. a company registered in Guernsey. Derbeyork has no beneficial interest in Reigndei Ltd and accordingly has not consolidated the results, assets and liabilities into its financial statements. Derbeyork holds these shares in trust for the beneficial owners: the 18 FCCs, MCC and the MCCA.'

No profit and loss account has ever been presented by DBY to Companies House since the company has been dormant and never traded. The ECB annual accounts disclose the insurance premiums and claims paid each year to the share holders. No RDL accounts are available for scrutiny to members of the public and the financial transactions are shrouded in mystery. My concerns centre upon the lack of disclosure in not only the MCC annual accounts but also those of several first-class counties such as Kent, Sussex and Nottinghamshire.

On September 25 2017 FORM DSO 1 was assigned by Tom Harrison (ceo the ECB) and Ian Lovett to strike Derbeyork trustees off the Companies House register. The ECB's solicitors submitted the application. Derbeyork Trustee Company Ltd was dissolved on January 2 2018. I decided to write to Harrison.

Dear Mr. Harrison

Jonathan Russell, the KPMG auditor of the latest ECB financial statement, has been in touch with ECB management following my enquiry concerning Reigndei Insurance Company Ltd. and the services it provides – see references below *.

I am a long-standing MCC member (elected playing member 1966) who was appointed by the MCC committee to serve on the Lord Griffiths Working Party responsible for the inauguration of the ECB and also more recently the WP responsible for the grant of the MCC Royal Charter. My concern centres upon the implications the Covid-19 pandemic might have on our future cricket at Lord's and whether adequate insurance cover has been provided for the loss of income on big match days this year.

I am aware that the Jockey Club and the All England Tennis Club (Wimbledon) bought the necessary cancellation insurance cover for major events but remain confused by the roles of the ECB/MCC in providing similar insurance cover at Lord's.

The response to my enquiry made through MCC states Reigndei Ltd. is a 'wholly owned subsidiary of the ECB who is the legal owner.' This is in contrast with the ECB statement that MCC is one of 20 beneficial owners that include the 18 FCCs and the MCCA. It would be helpful if you could explain this apparent contradiction, the actual function of Reigndei and the relationship that the ECB has with this insurance company. Do the transactions published in the financial statement note on p 41 include the necessary event cancellation insurance cover for loss of revenues associated with ticket sales, hospitality, retail and any other sales, at Lord's for 2020, on 'big match days' and covered by any ECB 'staging agreement' contractual obligations? I would be most grateful if you could supply me with the latest set of a/c's published by the ECB's wholly owned subsidiary Reigndei Ltd that record the counterparty transactions listed at para 20.4 of your latest ECB financial statement.

Thank you,
sincerely,
Nigel Knott (Dr.)

*Reference KPMG/MCC Communications
To: Nigel Knott 21/07/2020

Dear Nigel

As statutory auditor, I am not permitted to share such details as you have requested with other parties – however, I will contact management at the ECB as a follow-up to my previous referral.

I have been away from work for much of the last week, so as yet have not had the opportunity to discuss with my equivalent for the audit of MCC. I will do this later this week.

Kind Regards
Jonathan Russell

<Paul.Barron@kpmg.co.uk>
To: Nigel Knott

Dear Dr. Nigel Knot,

As Jonathan stated, as auditor it would not be appropriate for us to get involved in such communications on matters within the club's financial statements. However, I have spoken directly to the club on your behalf and they would be happy to respond to you. Please could you direct you queries straight to Guy Lavender, chief executive & secretary and Alastair Cameron, assistant secretary (finance). Their details are copied to this e-mail and they are expecting you to contact.

Regards, Paul.

Then I tried Ian Watmore, who was briefly the ECB chairman.

My enquiries as a long standing MCC playing member (1966) have failed to obtain the necessary answers and assuage my concerns. I am therefore questioning the wisdom of the 18 first-class counties, MCC and MCCA being involved vicariously via the ECB in offshore financial transactions that are shrouded in a blanket of secrecy? I expect from the governing body of our national sport and my own club, a Royal Charter Company, to have in place peerless standards of governance that include transparency and accountability.

In essence, my recent correspondence with the ECB financial director Scott Smith, who is a director of Reigndei Ltd. who I assume is registered with the ICAEW, has confirmed Reigndei Ltd to be a 'wholly owned subsidiary of the ECB.' This is in stark contrast to Companies House Records that (show) Derbyork Trustee Company Ltd. (No 2774287) was the legal owner of 100 per cent of the ordinary share capital of Reigndei Ltd. This also conflicts with the agm a/c's published by Kent and Sussex CC's declaring ownership of 30,000 shares each in Reigndei Ltd (Guernsey). If this is not confusing enough, I have to add the fact that the ceo of the ECB Tom Harrison became a director of Derbyork trustees in 2015 and the following year the person with significant control (PSC) who dissolved Derbyork in January 2018. What has happened since then to the Derbyork Trustee Co Ltd shares recorded in the Reigndei register of shareholders?

If Mr. Smith is correct then it appears that the ECB has annexed the original capital invested and the 585,000 shares (partly paid @95p per share) by the 18 FCC's, MCC and MCCA.

A detailed search of TCCB/ECB annual reports (1997 to date) reveals a cumulative total paid to Reigndei Ltd c £31m and claims being made by the ECB in excess of c £18m. These are considerable sums of money passing through an offshore bank account without any checks and balances being in place to ensure there is no possibility of fraud by allowing full third party (public) disclosure.

Mr. Smith considers these details to be confidential and not available to the public. KPMG, the ECB auditors, have refused to comment. The auditors of the MCC a/c's (KPMG) have also refused to comment.

This mysterious saga has been brought to a head by the failure of the cricket authorities to provide the necessary insurance cover for the cancellation of big match cricket events in 2020 and particularly at Lord's. Indeed, the responsibility for taking the necessary precautions in providing loss of income insurance policies similar to those arranged by the Jockey Club and the All England Tennis Club remains unresolved.

In the light of this information I would be most grateful if you will carry out a detailed investigation and respond to me with some answers, please, to the very obvious inconsistencies that exist and what appears to be a cover-up.

To: Alastair Cameron:

The KPMG auditors who were responsible for the ECB and MCC a/c's have referred me to you in connection with an offshore company, Reigndei Ltd.

At the annual meeting of 2006 I raised a question concerning this company and was informed by the club chairman that it was a company responsible for insuring against loss of ticket income from inclement weather conditions and a sum of £2m had been accumulated. I wrote to Keith Bradshaw, ceo MCC, to ask further questions about this offshore company and requested him to circulate my letter to the MCC committee. My questions remain unanswered and I am unable to trace any disclosure of what the ECB a/c's state is an MCC 'beneficial interest' in Reigndei Ltd.

Since the ECB has undergone a major restructuring in their governance procedures I believe they have decided to sever their links with Derbeyork Trustee Company Ltd. but still remain linked with Reigndei Ltd.

MCC is now a Royal Charter Company and I am very uneasy about the lack of transparency and accountability surrounding the MCC 'beneficial interest' being retained in an offshore company (Reigndei Ltd).

Can you please provide a full disclosure of the financial interests that my club purchased in Reigndei Ltd and any captive insurance claims that may arise from Covid?

Furthermore, would you be kind enough to break down the detail of the £2.251m 'rents rates and insurance' item six p 48 2019 a/c's.

Thank you,
Kind regards,
Nigel Knott (Dr.) Playing Member 27839

This Disclosure is made by Derbeyork Trustee Company Ltd Company No 02774287

'Derbeyork Limited is the legal owner of 100 per cent of the ordinary share capital of Reigndei Limited, a company registered in Guernsey. Derbeyork has no beneficial interest in the shares of Reigndei Limited and, accordingly, has not consolidated the results, assets and liabilities into its financial statements. Derbeyork Limited holds these shares in trust for the beneficial owners being the 19 first-class counties, Marylebone Cricket Club and the Minor Counties Cricket Association.'

From Alastair Cameron:
1. Reigndei Ltd is a wholly owned subsidiary of the England and Wales Cricket Board Ltd, so ECB is the legal owner,
2. Each of the first-class counties and MCC has a beneficial ownership in the entity but since Reigndei

was formed MCC has neither added capital to it nor received dividends,
3. ECB pays insurance premiums to Reigndei for cover and receives payments when claims are made,
4. ECB is required to have insurance for tickets for international fixtures in place as part of the staging agreement venues have with it; some of that insurance is placed with Reigndei and some is placed elsewhere in the market,
5. MCC has no management or operational involvement in Reigndei,
6. On that basis the club has never, since Reigndei was incorporated, felt it material to be disclosed in the accounts,
7. The £2.25m in the accounts is made up of business rates £1.6m, insurances £0.3m and rent payable in the Nursery ground £0.3m (the last item of which included an accrual based on the then latest estimate of the outcome of the rent review).
8. To reiterate, none of the £0.3m spend on insurance in 2019 relates to Reigndei.

Dear Alastair,

Thank you for your reply to my correspondence. Unfortunately, your answers in paras 1) and 2) seem to be in conflict. You state "Reigndei Ltd. is a wholly owned subsidiary of the ECB" followed by "MCC has a beneficial ownership in the entity."

Ownership is customarily established through the registration of deed of ownership (eg Land Register) or through a shareholding (company register) and in this case we know that MCC paid for a shareholding in RD and therefore a share certificate should have provided a receipt for the money and proof of ownership reflecting our club shareholding.

The involvement of the ECB as the owner remains a mystery. In the beginning, Derbeyork Trustee Company Ltd was constituted in order to place the original share capital (585,000) in Reigndei Ltd belonging to the 20 shareholders in trust. The DBY share capital amounted to 100 x £1 shares with three x shares being issued. DB Silk (MCC) was one of the three named trustees and a shareholder. The records of DBY held at Companies House show the annual accounts of DBY being submitted as a dormant company, finally being dissolved in 2018 by the person with significant control, the ceo ECB, Mr. T Harrison and Mr Ian Lovett acting in the capacity of two DBY Directors. Form DSO 01 was signed by them and submitted to Companies House to dissolve the company on September 25 2017. (This company was removed from the Companies House register on January 2 2018.)

Please inform me, who on behalf of MCC granted consent to dissolve DBY Trustee Company Ltd and what has happened to the shareholding in RD Ltd?

From: Scott Smith at ECB
Sent: 25 August 2020 10:05 am
To: Nigel Knott
Subject: Reigndei Ltd

Dear Nigel,

Thank you for your letter to Tom Harrison dated 21 August 2020, which he has passed onto me to respond directly to you.

Reigndei Ltd is a Guernsey based insurance captive for which ECB is the legal owner which holds shares in trust on behalf of the 18 FCCs, MCC and MCCA who are the beneficial owners of Reigndei. There is therefore no requirement for the ECB to reflect any ownership interest in our accounts.

Reigndei's function as an insurance captive for the game

is to provide the ECB, FCCs and MCC with rain cancellation insurance and early finish cover across both international and domestic fixtures.

The ticket cancellation insurance (for rain impacted or early finish international matches) is funded by the ECB and provided to all of our international venues as a condition of staging those matches. The ECB/Reigndei cover only extends to the 'ticket' element and Reigndei does not provide cover for other match day income streams that you reference (i.e. hospitality, retail etc) which would be each venue's responsibility to insure on the open market if deemed appropriate.

Reigndei also writes policies for T20 Blast matches against rain cancellation or rain impacted matches. These policies are written at the request and cost of the FCCs and MCC. FCCs and MCC are not obligated to purchase policies for rain cancellation from Reigndei and have the option of also placing their policies on the open market.

Given the relatively small size of Reigndei, ECB only ever places small layers of risk with the captive, whereby across a total of the £30m-£40m of total international ticket revenue in a given year, Reigndei will take on the 2nd layer of risk (after the ECB) of around £1m-£2.5m, with the balance circa £30m placed on the open market across a number of the world's largest underwriters.

The financial accounts for Reigndei Ltd are prepared pursuant to the Guernsey Financial Services Commission and are audited by BDO on a going concern basis. Day to day management of Reigndei is managed by Aon. Unfortunately we do not provide copies of Reigndei's accounts to the public.

I hope that provides you with the additional clarity you are after, if you have any further questions, please let me know.

Regards,
Scott
Scott Smith

Chief Financial Officer
England and Wales Cricket Board
Lord's Cricket Ground, St John's Wood, London, NW8 8QZ, England

To Bruce Carnegie-Bruce
Chairman MCC

My repeated attempt to obtain information concerning 30,000 £1 shares owned by MCC in an offshore Company Reigndei (Guernsey) Ltd. remains the subject of a steadfast refusal by the club secretariat to provide an answer.

The concerns I have expressed over the disappearance of our shareholding from the MCC annual accounts remains a mystery. My questions to AON Insurance Brokers, a Reigndei (Guernsey) shareholder, concerning the accounts, are rejected as "MCC" is required to make a valid request for information. There the circular tour ends as the MCC assistant secretary (finance) refuses to do so and my sincere concerns over possible fraudulent transactions remain outstanding.

The origins of the MCC shareholding in Reigndei (Guernsey) Ltd date back to when MCC, the 18 first-class counties and MCCA (now NCCA) purchased a total of 585,000 £1 Reigndei shares. Derbeyork Trustee Company Ltd (No 02774287), held these shares in trust until 02/01/2018, when the company was liquidated by the ceo ECB (T Harrison) who was the person who had assumed significant control. Many of the Company House returns in respect of this company seem to lack lawful authority.

The annual accounts of Kent and Sussex CC's each disclose shareholdings of 30,000 £1 shares in Reigndei (Guernsey) Ltd and declared them to be NIL value. The ECB in their annual accounts declare the financial transactions involving Reigndei (Guernsey) Ltd from which accumulated totals as at 2018 amount to a credit balance of c £15 million. The MCC shares have acquired significant capital appreciation since their issue.

There are many inconsistencies in the unaudited entries in the ECB accounts. In order to remove any possible suspicion of fraud, the bright sunlight needs to be shone upon the opaque financial transactions being purposefully hidden from view. As a very senior MCC member, I consider the actions of the secretariat in refusing an investigation to be unwise. Proper checks and balances with regular audits are an essential ingredient in best accounting practice. None have ever been carried out since Reigndei shares were first issued nearly 30 years ago.

This is proof of the shareholder interest in Reigndei (Guernsey) Ltd:

> The company is a wholly owned subsidiary of Derbeyork Trustee Company Limited, a company registered in England and Wales. Derbeyork Trustee Company Limited is itself owned by the 18 first-class cricket counties, MCC and the Minor Counties Cricket Association, which are governed by the England and Wales Cricket Board Limited, a company registered in England and Wales. The majority of the company's insurance business is undertaken with the related party disclosed above.
>
> The deep discount security issued by one of the members of the Derbeyork Trustee Company Limited was settled in the prior year (see note 1).
>
> The Kent and Sussex CC's annual accounts include a note that their shares in RDL are of nil value. Notts CC include a note in their accounts that the shareholding in RDL has been 'written off.' The question arises as to why copies of the annual accounts of an offshore company in

Guernsey (RDL) are not supplied to all its shareholders and PWC (ECB auditor and MCC auditor) and MCC seek to cover-up any details.

What we know from a trawl of the ECB annual accounts since 31/12/1997 – 31/12/2020 : Premiums paid to RDL = £34.559m and claims receivable from RDL = £20.036m, leaving a credit balance of £14.523m.

This equates to a value of £24.32p per share x 30,000 MCC shares as at 31/12/2020. Hence £729,600 should have appeared in the MCC annual accounts but there is no trace of this.

In 2016/2017 £7.706m claims were receivable against £3.382m payable = £3.324m surplus or £5.50p per share.

These are large sums of money with no checks and balances available for examination.

The extraordinary confusion and obfuscation can only be addressed with a detailed disclosure of all RDL transactions in the possession of the ECB.

No dividends have ever been paid, so how have the shareholders such as MCC benefitted?

Why was the chief executive of the ECB appointed the person with significant control of DBY and allowed to strike DBY off the company register to enable the ECB to become the owner of the 595,000 RDL shares? Nobody has ever been able to provide a simple answer to the simple question – why are the registered RDL shareholders not disclosing their ownership in their annual accounts?

Yours sincerely
Nigel Knott

The principal question that remains without answers was left hanging in the cricketing air.

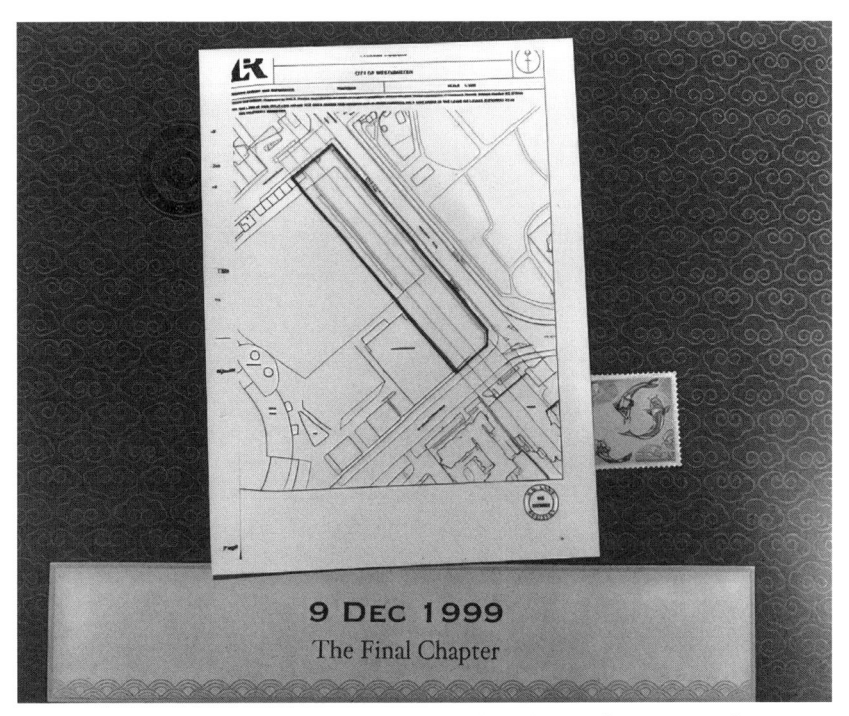

*The area at the Nursery End of Lord's within Wellington Road
that denotes the disused tunnels*

Sketch design – creating a landmark corner for Lord's

Nigel Knott visiting No. 10 Downing Street

Larry the Cat

Current Prison Wall of the Nursery End, implication of keep out!

David Morley plan with a magnificent opportunity to create a sense of arrival entrance for guests

"The MCC Development Committee enters via the Disgrace Gates."

Chapter 6 – Tunnels and a Train Crash
A disastrous auction decision – the loss of Lord's property

Chapter 6
Tunnels and a Train Crash

In schoolboy understanding, the decision to purchase the disused railway tunnels within the Lord's estate at the Nursery End should have been a 'no brainer' for MCC in 1999. This did not occur. It could well be said that this was the worst strategic decision. and indeed the most expensive decision, in the club's history. As a consequence of being outbid, the club would not have any development rights to this cavernous and well-preserved area, although it would retain control of the 18 inches of topsoil. The strip of land runs alongside but within Wellington Road and extends to 179 metres in length by 38 metres depth. The two Victorian tunnels were owned by Railtrack, and the line itself, running from Marylebone to Aylesbury, had not been used since the nationwide Beeching cuts were imposed in 1966. The arched brickwork was in good condition and yet the entire space, 1.66 acres in total and running underneath the Nursery ground, seemed to be of scant use to MCC.

Railtrack wanted £1.75m for it. But MCC, having recently overspent on the media centre (a building that seems to be admired far more by those who don't work in it) had an overdraft of around £15m and were uncomfortable with further borrowing. As a result, they dithered. Railtrack took the land to auction. MCC stopped bidding at £2.35m and Charles Rifkind, a barrister turned property developer who lived locally and walked past Lord's most days, prevailed with a bid of £2.35m.

As an ordinary member I felt bound to express my opinion at the time in e-mail correspondence with the president, Tony Lewis. I suggested a sum of more than £5m should be considered as a possible knock-out blow to any opposition. This was bringing back memories of 1860 when Lord's was sold by the Eyre estate to Isaac Moses for £7,000. That year, MCC's committee failed to bid at auction for the freehold of Lord's cricket ground. Railtrack had advertised its land being for sale at auction on December 9 1999.

This was a very busy time for the club's management, with three working parties in place at the same time: A staging agreement working party (chaired by Charles Fry); a members' liaison group (chaired by the president) and the Sir Michael Jenkins structure working party 'Preparing for the future' comprised of Fry, Oliver Stocken, Anthony Wreford and Philip Hodson.

I was serving on the first two at the time and Roger Knight, the secretary, was the common link between all three. It was

Maurice Putsman, the lawyer who advised Charles Rifkind on the purchase of the disused tunnels at Lord's

less than two weeks before the news reached me of the Railtrack auction and I was immediately in touch with him and Lewis:

Dear Roger,

I have to tell you that I am fed up with nagging about the total lack of communication over the TMG's staging agreement. It is now more than 12 months since the MCC SWP last met and I have made numerous telephone calls in the meantime to keep abreast of events with Charles Fry and Robert Griffiths. I have also been in touch with Tony Lewis to express to him my disappointment over the handling of the affair in the newsletter (amongst other things where this publication is concerned). It seems quite extraordinary that in response to my agm resolution, the president set up a SWP to look into this whole affair – we made an amazing breakthrough in a short space of time with the formation of the TMG consortium and since then there has been little attempt to communicate back on a regular basis. I understand from Tony that he has asked you to address this matter and cannot give me an answer as to why you have not acted in accordance with his wishes. I have tried on numerous occasions to contact Robert Griffiths and have left messages to 'phone me back but without success. There are many members who are asking me what is going on and I have no idea – but then I am only a member of the SAWP and the MLG!

Roger, how much longer do we have to put up with this secrecy, lack of communication and inefficiency because I am pretty fed up. Why cannot things be done properly? Nigel.

Two days later the newspapers announced the club had failed to buy the freehold land at the Nursery End. I was left shocked and even more so when I learned how little the club was prepared to bid.

Sent 13/12/99 @ 10.34pm by Nigel Knott

Dear Tony,

Following my e-mail sent to you on November 29 1999 you kindly asked Michael Blow to contact me direct. I made it clear to him the land being sold by Railtrack should be purchased **at any price** as it had to be worth more to the club than any outside interest. It was my expressed view that a TOP-CLASS professional should be employed and briefed on the club's behalf to purchase at any price. It seems incredible to me the committee had put a price on this priceless piece of land equal to the glass and plastic abortion that now stands upon it. Just mark my words – nothing but trouble lies ahead with an outsider having bought a significant interest within our walls. The committee's extraordinary valuation beggars belief, I did say to you that **£5m might have to be paid**. In these circumstances commercial valuations are irrelevant when our control over the WHOLE ground is of paramount importance. I do not know what the membership will say but you can expect more ructions for a certainty. I do not speak with hindsight but think the committee has made yet another blunder of Titanic proportions with perhaps the most serious implications yet. I have spoken to Robert Griffiths this evening and he tells me he is on record as expressing an identical view to mine at the last estates sub-committee meeting – is nobody listening? He tells me also that nobody told him of the outcome of the auction until we spoke earlier this evening. Perhaps nobody dares to face the music! Whoever has bought this land must be rubbing their hands with glee – the fact they have outbid us tells me we have missed a pretty big trick here. Will anyone be called to account? Sincerely, Nigel.

No reply was received and so I sent a reminder to Lewis:

Dear Tony,

I have the following scenario in mind – is it pure fantasy? A property company has bought the freehold at Lord's with the intention of holding the club to ransom and offering to sell the title to us for a quick buck at some future date. There could of course be one or two influential MCC members in the background in place as willing partners who are also hoping to benefit. I find it difficult to believe that the committee has been caught napping yet again. It is unfortunate that my knowledge of the recent history at Lord's brings these unhappy thoughts to mind – you will I hope inform me that I am living in the realms of unreality.

Best wishes, Nigel.

Lewis responded:

Have a happy Christmas. I am just out of the front door, off to Cape Town.

Nobody was caught napping over the Railtrack sale. The pre-planning was serious and wide-ranging. Even at the auction we had our own incognito MCC member ready to top the best offer and sell it back to us if that would help hold down the price. The best man to answer your doubts is Maurice de Rohan. He led us in the work.

I am sure you have heard that last Tuesday's meeting was a success. The reforms are on the move. They will be with the MLG by mid-January. Roger met a whiz-kid on websites – introduced by David Medway – last Friday. I am due to meet ICC in South Africa to work out a proposal for an MCC role, if they think it worthwhile. We shall see.

It is going to be a fine New Year… believe me!

Best wishes Tony

Tony's fine New Year arrived and the Jenkins report was published – he himself was to become club chairman and Roger Knight was to be the chief executive officer – incredible. Lewis was very unhappy when I asked him how much the secretary was to be paid in his new role. I was told to MYOB!

I had a further disagreement with the president when I sent him a fax three months later, in March 2000, to tell him how disappointed I was that he had succumbed to committee pressure and disbanded the members liason group. I told him that the latest minutes were incorrect. I said that "the whole mlg initiative of yours has been completely undermined by a few disloyal committee members who bitterly opposed your course of action in the first place."

Lewis was now in Australia and moving on to India on Wales Tourist Board business. "My wife was upset to read an aggressive fax from you at home. I will leave you to your fantasies of 'enemies within' and in turn I would be happy if you will leave me with the propagation of my reforms.

"The remainder of my MCC presidency is going to be spent at our cricket games or golf days or functions of club importance. Certainly it will not be spent answering aggressive strictures from you or others as I have done with some tolerance over the past 18 months. Direct them to the chief executive or the chairman."

I was to have no further dealings with Lewis when his year as president came to an end and we never bumped into each other at Lord's. I was saddened to learn, a quarter of a century later, of the decline in his health.

Lewis was no property expert (and could not be expected to be) but others within the club he had entrusted with the task of securing the disused tunnels were most certainly not, either. Charles Rifkind, a local property developer. arrived at the Nursery ground entrance to Lord's to visit his prize, which amounted to owning the head lease. He was immediately treated as a malign influence carrying tares and contact with him had to be avoided at any cost. That was until the new secretary/ceo Keith Bradshaw arrived in 2006. Keith's experience in the commercial world with Price Waterhouse and Deloitte's made him an excellent choice. As one of his predecessors, Jack Bailey, had emphasised, making a profit at Lord's was almost unheard of.

*

Bradshaw's arrival at Lord's had brought me new optimism. He was somebody I considered to be very much an MCC members secretary. He came at a crucial time and was only the second appointee whom I would describe in such a way since the departure of Jack Bailey. In between came a retired army officer in John Stephenson followed by a retired schoolmaster in Roger Knight, both with little understanding of commerce.

Bradshaw was a very different secretary/ceo whose professional qualifications made him an ideal candidate to replace Knight. A first-class cricketer from 'Down Under' with the additional benefit of being a qualified chartered accountant who had a commercial brain, he had a friendly, open approach and listened to rank-and-file members and others as well as to the committee. His concern was quickly apparent over some of the long-standing governance problems at Lord's – none more pressing than Bailey's WP having reported in 1984 on 'the wholly unsatisfactory return on the club's investment in facilities at Lord's.'

Nothing has changed for the better in this respect despite Bradshaw's Herculean efforts. Burgeoning increases in member subscriptions have always been the order of the day at agms to plug numerous 'black holes' in the club's accounts. In effect annual subscriptions have become cash calls to cover perennial trading losses. He grasped the governance issues he faced very quickly. Sorting out the mess proved to be quite another story. The task proved to be impossible.

As Bradshaw's successor, Derek Brewer, put it to the ISWP in a paper in 2014, MCC 'is dysfunctional.'

Having spent a small fortune on planning development at Lord's through the 'Vision' and employing world class architects, the chairman and treasurer of MCC throughout much of Bradshaw's time in charge, Oliver Stocken and Justin Dowley, experienced what can only be described as a cerebral malfunction. At the last moment in 2011 they decided to address the MCC committee with a "back us or sack us" proposal to cancel the £400m 'Vision' development plan. What is interesting is the fact that Stocken had replaced Charles Fry as chairman of MCC a year before his term in office expired. Was this a harbinger of things to come?

Bradshaw had recognised the importance of Charles Rifkind, the new freeholder and landlord, at an early stage. He saw him not as a threat but as a partner and friend to be included in the opportunity to unlock the huge potential value of Lord's. Rifkind also owns three properties within the Lord's estate (the MCC owns four) accessible from Grove End Road on the western boundary. A holistic approach to ground development was, to Bradshaw, another no-brainer. But he failed to take into account the possibility of stratagems and spoils being plotted by members of his own team and the flagrant abuses of power exposed in the final day of reckoning.

The summary intervention of the club chairman and treasurer came as a shattering blow to many in 2011 when the whole 'Vision' project was abandoned. Sir John Major, one of the supporters of the project and a key member of the development committee, made his feelings clear in a letter to the president dated March 2 2012. He felt he had been traduced. He has played no part in MCC affairs since. For his part, Bradshaw felt he had been stabbed in the back. He resigned as ceo later that same year and returned to Australia with this debacle perhaps playing a part in his tragic final illness. He died of bone cancer in 2021.

A rational explanation for the clash at committee level over the 'Vision' concept is difficult to give. Yet there is

Compton and Edrich stands with no roofs and encroaching on the Nursery Ground. Having no sympathy to the residential environment as seen from the Wellington Road

Robin Ebdon was responsible for the appointment and build of these Compton and Edrich stands

plenty of evidence that may suggest malicious intent and a steadfast refusal to accept Rifkind as a trusted partner at Lord's in a deluded attempt to deprive him of potential significant profit from his investment. There were also many in the inner circle, including an influential behind-the-scenes assistant secretary, who clearly preferred piecemeal development of Lord's over decades, financed from scarce club funds, giving the club control and denying Rifkind any benefit. Lack of commercial judgement! Since then, the Compton and Edrich Stands have been built without any roof and the footprint of these stands extends into the playing area of the Nursery End, rendering the continuation of adult cricket impossible.

What is not generally known is the fact that Bradshaw arranged to meet Rifkind soon after his arrival to understand why no discussions had taken place on ground development. With a landowner within the Lord's estate, he found it very strange that nobody had been in contact with him.

Commercial negotiations began within an atmosphere of trust and a talented development committee team in place, briefed to explore the exciting possibility of residential development along the Wellington Road boundary. A relationship based upon an equal footing soon resulted with Rifkind offering to contribute monthly payments in settlement of MCC's monthly Invoices for expenditure on planning, legal, construction and architects pre-construction. These payments averaged roughly £100.000 per month (ref Invoice October 2008) that amounted to a total c £1m.

Bradshaw lost no time in seizing the opportunity to establish a trusted relationship with Rifkind and forming a development committee that included Sir John Major, the former prime minister; Sir Scott Baker, a high court judge; Lord Grabiner QC, a Labour peer, and the former England captains Michael Atherton and Tony Lewis. Robert Griffiths QC, a Welsh barrister who might have had an international rugby career but for one Gareth Edwards taking his place at scrum half in Wales' junior teams, was appointed as chairman.

In a letter to Rifkind on December 18 2008 Bradshaw wrote:

M.C.C. MASTERPLAN FOR LORD'S GROUND

I refer to recent discussions on how best to progress matters regarding the masterplan and to your joint involvement in the process. On behalf of MCC I would confirm our agreement, in principle, to move forward with the following understanding:

1. A 50:50 financial arrangement to seek planning consent for the masterplan and share, equally, the rewards from a redeveloped Wellington Road end.
2. MCC to lead the overall planning process, but with responsibility for detail and design of the residential element to be provided by Rifkind Levy Partnership (this referred to Rifkind's then partner Jonathan Levy).
3. All costs to be shared 50:50 as per the attached budget updated September 25 2008.

As proposed, I would confirm that the committee and any other relevant committee will be kept fully informed of progress and I will continue to ensure that, where appropriate, you are made aware of both their conclusions and any reservations, as soon as any arise. I would also confirm our agreement to continue to run the bank account in the name of MCC with both parties contributing a sum of £100,000, and a mutual agreement to top up these funds as required, to ensure a continuing credit balance of not less than £200,000.

We envisage that this letter and your signed acknowledgement will record the commitment to work together in this process. Hopefully, we will end up with an agreed masterplan, a planning strategy and a detailed heads of agreement for a development agreement that can be put to the MCC committee and subsequently, if approved, to the members. If the masterplan, the planning strategy and the final agreed heads of agreement between us are approved by the members we can then document the detailed development agreement.

As ever, we are approaching this in the utmost good faith, as I know you both are. However, this letter records MCC's present intent and is not intended to be legally binding and is written without liability for MCC or any officer, member or employee of MCC.

Let us see if we can deliver something truly outstanding for all. I should be grateful if you would signify your acceptance of the terms set out in this letter by signing the enclosed copy and returning it to me.

Yours sincerely
Signed   Keith Bradshaw
Secretary Chief Executive MCC

Yet by 2011 the 'Vision for Lord's' as it had been termed by Bradshaw and others, was no more. Stocken, supported by Dowley, cited financial risk at the onset of a world recession. But where had "the utmost good faith" gone?

Ten years on from having initiated the proposed redevelopment, Bradshaw wrote a further letter.

"As we approach the tenth anniversary of the first publication of the development plans we should reflect that whilst the passage of time has not yet yielded this development, it has afforded us the perspective of a lost opportunity.

If a different decision had been made in 2008, and

the scheme, which had been unanimously supported by the MCC ground development committee, including Sir John Major, had been allowed to proceed, then Lord's would deservedly be sitting amongst the world's best-in-class sporting venues, would have significant financial resources and would have perhaps removed itself from the burden of a rental liability. We would ask you to be tolerant of the exact design of the Herzog & de Meuron scheme. To some extent it was merely to inform and masterplan the potential opportunity. Without question, what is clear is that emphasis will be placed on the delivery of high quality architecture and design. Lord's, the location and its international significance demands it.

Let us remember the boldness of vision from previous committees which led to the commissioning of the media centre and its construction by boat builders in Cornwall. At some point in the future we hope that the committee will embrace the same confidence of purpose to profitably reshape the future of their club."

Keith Bradshaw, the first Australian to run MCC. An innovative and very popular secretary and chief executive. He supported the Vision for Lord's, much to the annoyance of his chairman Oliver Stocken, he had a trying time ...

Charles Rifkind (left) with Keith Hague, chief executive of Wellington Hospital, in the disused railway tunnels at Lord's

Sir Philip Beck, chairman of Railtrack when the disused tunnels were sold in 1999

Charles Rifkind (left) with David Gower, cricketer and commentator

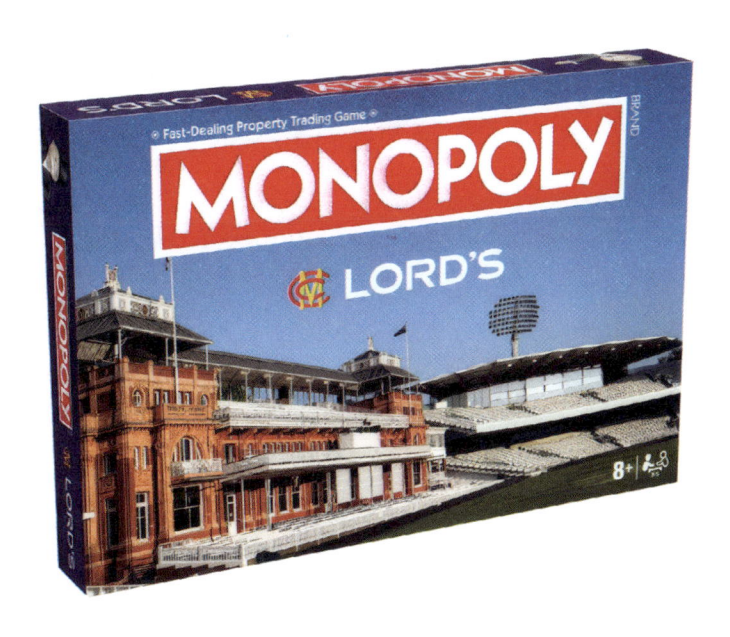

The new game in town: Lord's Monopoly

"Aye, Jim lad, we set sail for Lord's cricket ground on the next tide."

Chapter 7 – What Is the Point of MCC?
A real estate Treasure Trove at Lord's

Chapter 7
What Is the Point of MCC?

Another extraordinary window of opportunity still exists to right the wrongs of the past. The management mishandling in 2024 of the redevelopment of the Tavern and Allen Stands was truly shambolic and this should have awoken even the most sycophantic MCC members. It will require a huge leap of faith for the membership to accept past failures and for the club's committee to swallow personal pride and to accept it does not have the sovereign powers to do no wrong. The committee's duty should still be to act in the best interests of members.

The choice of this book's title *Tunnel Vision at Lord's* is not what might easily be described as a parody based upon one catastrophic incident at Lord's involving Railtrack, but something much more that is deeply rooted in the historical psyche or soul of MCC. Perhaps a syndrome might be a better description for a deep-seated malaise with a cerebral origin as there is a long history of committee failures that are difficult to interpret within the powers of reason and common sense.

The aphorisms 'far sighted' and 'short sighted' are commonly used to describe otherwise long-term economic choices or poor and ill-conceived short-term botched plans. In this example of MCC governance, amaurosis may be a better term to describe a form of cerebral blindness. The introduction of the development project raised hopes amongst a few optimists. What went so badly wrong? Their opinions are supported by fact and not to be summarily dismissed. It is difficult to understand why a Royal Charter Company such as MCC has never taken any remedial action to redress the obvious fatal flaws in governance.

So to the point Quentin Letts raised on BBC Radio 4 in asking: "What is the point of MCC?" The fact he did not know whether the club was resisting the economic and global forces of modernity or leading the charge of change was itself a telling admission. The programme was disappointing because the question remained unanswered.

I will attempt to remedy the situation as the question is a good one. None of the Radio 4 contributors, who ranged from past captains of the England male and female XIs to an American journalist, was able to resolve the conundrum. It could be said that MCC has been left as a naked emperor without any clothes ever since it was forced to hand over the governance of our game to the TCCB in 1968. However, MCC still owns (most of) Lord's, the laws of cricket and if nothing else, it remains the conscience of cricket together with being the trustee and guardian of its best interests and finest traditions.

At a time of burgeoning monetisation within the ranks of nearly all our national games, cricket needs an urgent injection of the good old-fashioned grass roots amateur spirit which MCC has historically provided. The club has the biggest fixture list of any club in the UK and a long history of generously funding the grass roots game at school, club and university level both in the UK and overseas. No club is better placed to play a formal role up to u-16 level. Traditional cricket has long been recognised as a civilising influence on society and the celebrated historian George Trevelyan once wrote that if the French nobility had only played cricket with their servants, they would not have had their chateaux burned down!

The public perception of MCC does contain an element of truth. The members kicked and screamed against the introduction of female membership and still resist the radical makeover in constitutional government it so badly needs.

Today the club suffers from a lack of leadership and direction, personal conflicts of interest and what is a major conflicted interest with the ECB. There is a strong smell of nepotism at Lord's. It is worth quoting Geoffrey Moorhouse, who wrote an excellent book on Lord's: "Hardly any differences of opinion exist between the MCC committee and the TCCB on major issues affecting the conduct and playing of cricket. They share the same stance on a whole range of cricketing matters. So frequently, however, are individuals to be found with one foot placed firmly in each camp, that it is rather difficult to avoid the suspicion that the long debate has not really been about the ideal structure of administration at all. It may have been about that primitive pastime of human beings jostling for power." Nothing has changed.

Sir John Major and Lord Grabiner highlighted what they considered to be significant inadequacies in the management and governance of MCC that needed to be remedied as a matter of urgency. The ingredients of the Lord's development dispute can be accessed at *https://www.channel4.com/news/critics-hit-out-at-mcc-over-shelved-plans-for-lords*.

A statement from the club said the former prime minister had quit the committee in 2011 "because of fundamental disagreements over the direction of policy on the 'Vision for Lord's,' the manner in which decisions have been reached, and their wider implications for the club." This was patently untrue and was immediately challenged by Major, who registered his displeasure.

The then president, Philip Hodson, responded (publicly): "Further to my letter to members on February 13 2012, Sir John Major did not think my words reflected the true reasons for his resignation. Whilst he is in favour of a development at the Nursery End, the abandonment of this project in November 2011 was not the cause of his resignation; rather it was the flawed process which led to this decision. Accordingly, since the agenda for the annual meeting will include a discussion and vote on the committee's decision not to accept proposals for residential development on the club's leasehold land, I have agreed to attach Sir John's' letter of March 2."

From Sir John Major:

"I have read your letter of February 13, addressed to all full and senior members of MCC. Whilst I am grateful for your kind words about my contribution to the club, I fear that your letter totally misrepresents the reason for my resignation from the main committee. You wrote: '… the committee agreed that the preservation of Lord's as a cricket ground was more important than a windfall of cash. Of equal importance was the committee's belief that members would not be inclined to accept such a scheme. This stance led to the resignation from the committee of Sir John Major.'

This –emphatically– is not true. If I may, I will repeat (some of) the points made in my resignation letter to the chairman, dated December 9 2011.

I did not resign over the decision to abandon the 'Vision for Lord's,' even though I believe it is a serious mistake the club may come to regret. I resigned due to the manner in which this decision was reached.

During the last four years we have spent a huge amount of time, energy – and cost – discussing the 'Vision for Lord's,' which was endorsed by the main committee on many occasions – often overwhelmingly, but sometimes with a minority of very committed opponents.

I sat on the development committee for the 'Vision' until the main committee was informed that our work was done. It was disbanded. Since our work was not done, the decision came as a surprise to me and other members of the development committee. However, in the interests of harmony, I accepted this. When a new committee, the 'masterplan working party,' was subsequently set up, I was reassured when Sir Michael Jenkins – who chaired the working party which had developed the original 'Vision for Lord's' – was included as a member. Yet this committee was disbanded without ever meeting.

A 'ground working party' was then formed to carry matters forward. The composition of its membership was entirely biased against the plans in the 'Vision.' As the chairman of the working party conceded to me in committee, this working party contained only opponents of the scheme: not one single member had ever expressed any support for the comprehensive development of Lord's.

Nonetheless, I was hopeful they would take an open-minded look at the wider opportunities offered but – as I ascertained in committee – they failed to even discuss any outcome other than a piecemeal redevelopment over many years, funded from our own resources.

Moreover, the argument put forward in the working party report was tendentious. We were told we might not get planning consent; that the additional seats could not be filled; and that the members of the club were moving against a residential scheme at the Nursery End (whereas in the past we had been advised precisely the opposite). It seemed as though this report had been drafted in such a way as to justify a pre-determined outcome. As a result, the working party report unceremoniously ditched many years of work on the 'Visión for Lord's.' I concede, of course, that the committee has every right to change its mind – even as comprehensively as it has done. But this episode has been damaging – to the MCC purse, and our reputation. This is not the way our club should be run.

The converse is, I believe, that we have missed an opportunity to raise an absolute minimum of £50m for the club, which would have greatly strengthened our financial resources; enabled us to improve facilities for members and hold (or even reduce) their annual fees in what is a very difficult economic climate; and make, if we wished, a larger contribution than at present to the wider world of cricket.

I do not argue for the maximum 'Vision,' since economic times have changed, and we have to take account of this: this is why I agreed that removing the 'undercroft' from the scheme was sensible. But I do believe a plan could – and should – have been approved that would not have changed the ambience of the ground.

I agree with those members who argue that we are first and foremost a cricket club. But this argues for a sensitive development of Lord's, not for the lengthy, fragmented approach that now seems to be in operation.

When I resigned from the committee I did so after much deliberation, and with very great reluctance. At that time, the chairman asked me not to circulate my resignation letter to members of the main committee, nor to make any public comment. In the interests of MCC I agreed and have remained true to my word.

However, although I have kept my counsel, others have not. I have found the reason for my resignation repeatedly misrepresented in the media, and now in your letter to members. It gives the impression that I did believe cash was more important that the preservation of Lord's whereas this is not, and never has been, my view. Unsurprisingly, such an impression has generated a reaction from people who have been misled. At the time of my resignation, I told the chairman – orally and in writing – that, if my position was traduced, I would not hesitate to correct the record.

It is for that reason that I am copying this letter to all members of the main committee and would ask that you copy it to all full and senior members. That way, there can be no further doubt about the reason behind my resignation, nor my personal and lasting commitment to MCC and the wider world of cricket."

Lord Grabiner, sacked from the development committee, questioned the decision to shelve any redevelopment of the world's most famous cricket ground and said the decision-making process lacked transparency. He told Channel 4 news: "It is driven in my view by entirely wrong motives. I think we all know that if you run organisations as if they were in your hip pocket, ordinary governance rules simply don't apply."

The club responded to the criticism by saying: "MCC has always made it clear that the project was subject to both the financial viability of the proposed development as a whole and reaching an agreement with the ECB on the number of major matches to be played at Lord's in the coming years. The club has not ruled out any development at the Nursery End in the future."

Nick Gandon, who instigated a special general meeting of MCC and subsequently joined the club's committee

Grabiner's letter was read out by Sir Simon Robertson at a special meeting convened in October 2013 through the requisitionists, led by Nick Gandon, a former director of the Cricket Foundation, and Paddy Briggs, a long-standing MCC member. The resolution was: 'That the committee, in consultation with the requisitionists of this resolution and other MCC members, appoints an independent panel to seek evidence about and to report its findings and recommendations to members on the following:

The processes followed by the committee which led to a decision to reject an intended offer of £100m from Almacantar Limited made in the context of the 'Vision for Lord's' and the development of the club's leasehold land – and the rationale for this decision;

The value of the intended offer in the light of the club's current and forecast future financial situation;

In the light of (a) and (b) the appropriateness of any changes as to how the short-term and long-term management of ground development activity at Lord's is organised and conducted – and any other matters relevant thereto.'

Writing to Derek Brewer, Bradshaw's successor as secretary of MCC, they said: "A financial windfall of £110m is a 'game changer' for MCC that would provide the capital necessary not only to fund the redevelopment of stands and facilities, but also procure a club unencumbered with debt for the benefit of current and future generations of members. For reasons that have never been clearly established, MCC's committee terminated discussions with Almacantar and withdrew from the process in November 2011. In doing so, it has not only declined a windfall, but declined to remove extensive long-term rental liabilities."

Nevertheless, the membership, as it often tended to do, sided with the committee and the motion was comfortably quashed. This only appeared to emphasise, once again, that most MCC members took only a passing interest in events beyond the boundary – so long as they were able to watch the best matches in the best seats.

Grabiner, who as with his fellow QC, Griffiths, had given a great deal of his expertise gratis, was an exception. In his letter he said: "I attended all the meetings of the development committee and I have a good memory of the events. At all times we had the benefit of advice from three independent professionals. In May 2010 the development committee was in effect down to a much smaller group of eight in the hope that more rapid progress would be achieved. The key points that I would like to draw to the attention of MCC members are as follows:

The two key MCC officers, Oliver Stocken (chairman) and Justin Dowley (treasurer) were absolutely opposed to the 'Vision' and the task which was supposed to be performed by the development committee. Both were members of the smaller group and at all times they took every opportunity to try to deflect the group from that task by engaging debate about what they claimed were the deficiencies of the 'Vision.'

Mike Hussey of Almacantar, the favoured development partner for the 'Vision for Lord's'

In fact that was not our job. It was recognised by everyone else at the table that when a suitable partner had been identified, it would be necessary for the development committee and MCC to sit down with the chosen developer in order to formulate a planning application to be made to Westminster Council. The planning application needed the approval of MCC and would have to work in all respects, including financially.

Oliver and Justin were, and I believe still are, motivated by a strong sense of irritation driven by the fact that in 1999, when the strip of land within Lord's adjacent to the Wellington Road was put up for auction by Railtrack it was purchased by the Rifkind Levy Partnership (RLP) rather than by MCC. I have no personal knowledge of the 1999 events but the talk around the club – and I know this view is shared by people with first-hand knowledge —is that the then estates committee made a bad error by not authorising a higher offer. Indeed, I believe the 1999 documents show that Railtrack offered the land to MCC before putting it to auction but for some unfathomable reason the offer was ignored or declined.

As a result, I believe that Oliver and Justin proceeded at all times on a deeply flawed basis. Instead of focusing exclusively on the correct question, namely, how should the development committee best proceed by reference to the interests of the club, they were rather more concerned to sweep under the carpet the abject failings of the estates committee. I believe these gentlemen have failed to discharge their duties to MCC and why, in a television interview, I called for their resignation.

They both suggested that to proceed with the project would involve grave financial risk for the club. Yet it was never the task of the development committee to evaluate the 'Vision': its job was to find a suitable development partner and then, together, they would scrutinise the plans and make any appropriate amendments to it before submitting a planning application. As to the financial risk, I believe this was scaremongering because the proposal put forward to Almacantar as the selected developer made plain that they, and not the club, would bear that risk.

In a palpable attempt to divert the attention of MCC members away from the debate about the potential development inside Wellington Road – this area is and always has been an eyesore, and a large underused part of the estate – Stocken focused on possible piecemeal improvements elsewhere in the ground. As a result of all these machinations the development committee proceeded at a snail's pace but eventually identified five leading developers. It was satisfied (again unanimously) with the choice of Almacantar on the basis it had the necessary expertise and financial clout (backed by, among others, the Agnelli family) to be the partner of MCC. No explanation has ever been provided as to why two highly reputable developers thought it appropriate to submit non-conforming proposals. Given all the circumstances, members may feel able to draw their own conclusions as to what went on behind the scenes at the time. For my part it left a nasty taste.

Thereafter, the development committee and the subsequent assembled smaller group which was supposed to take its place were, without more ado, informed that they had been disbanded. Common sense suggests they would have been better left in place to monitor the progress of discussions between Almacantar and the club. Instead, a masterplan working group was set up in May 2011 to perform this monitoring task. My understanding is that there were negotiations with Almacantar which were conducted by Stocken but this new group was never involved: indeed, I believe it never met, even once. The negotiations came to nothing.

This is a depressing story for cricket lovers because it reveals a scandalous state of affairs as far as the governance of MCC is concerned. Decision making is done in a high-handed, undemocratic and secretive fashion by one or two people and the potential damage to the club and cricket generally is enormous. It is a matter of public record that Sir John Major resigned from the main committee because he was unhappy with the procedures which had been adopted on this important matter. He would not lightly have taken this step. A key aspect of the whole sorry story is that the vast majority of members are wholly ignorant of what has been going on because the details have been suppressed."

Robertson said that he had been concerned for some time about the polarised position of MCC and the requisitionists, but did not think the club had given members enough information on any potential development to make an informed judgment. He had suggested to the chairman that independent committees be established to evaluate development possibilities and review the governance of MCC, which was not of an acceptable standard, but the chairman had declined to accept his suggestion.

Mr. A.J.B. Oakes, a member, said that members had been told that the club could not afford to purchase the land in 1999, but, if it had done so, it would now have an asset worth £320m. If the freehold and leasehold interests were merged, the £320m would be shared between the freeholder and the leaseholder and would produce an assured sum of £160m to the club to fund whatever it wished, and all the risk would be taken by the developer rather than by the club. A cautious assumption was that the annual rent was likely to rise to about £250,000 a year backdated to 2012.

Stocken, for his part, said that he was flabbergasted by Grabiner's letter, of which he had been unaware until it was read out. They were all members of the finest cricket club in the world, he added, they all loved Lord's and they had a duty to take the best possible care of it for future generations and for cricket as a whole; they also had to do everything possible to maximise their chances of winning major matches, especially over the next two years.

He agreed that it would have been better to have bought the leasehold strip in 1999, but at that time the club had bank debts and loans of more than £5m, so had considered it unwise to bid higher than £2.35m. Instead, the club had been able to carry out major refurbishments on or below budget. He said that four choices had been available – to allow residential development on the leasehold strip, to carry out residential development on the club's own land, to develop the land from the club's own resources or to do nothing. It was wrong to suggest that the group that had been formed did not look at all possible options: no restrictions had been placed on it. He said that doing nothing was not a sensible option. The ECB required deficiencies in certain facilities to be remedied, but residential development on the club's land was problematical and not financially viable.

In November 2011, the ground working party advised the committee to reject Almacantar's offer to develop the Nursery End because 'significant strings' were attached.

Brian McGowan, a member of the development committee, recorded his emotions: "I have been in business for 50 years and I have never experienced anything like this. I have not spoken to Tony Grabiner for several weeks and there is no collusion or connivance between us, but I agree with everything he says. This process is a disgrace and to hide behind the argument that this is how private clubs operate is inaccurate and if true it is about time they and in particular MCC changed their ways.

"The development committee was later slimmed down to a smaller negotiating group that included the club and the finance committee chairmen. Eventually this smaller group put forward a recommendation which after a lengthy debate was agreed. Doubts were expressed by a minority who received safeguards and assurances to ensure there was unanimity on the committee to proceed with Almacantar. Part of this agreement was that we would amend the original 'Vision' to include changed circumstances, financial constraints and good ideas proposed by the other bidders. There was always the obligation that the final agreement had to be approved by the finance and main committees.

"What has happened since beggars belief. Just about

everything that had been agreed has been overturned to the extent there is a real risk of losing Almacantar altogether. Any talk of avoiding any payment to Rifkind would only result in a cheap sub-standard alternative that future generations of MCC members would quite rightly find appalling. As I have said before, there is an unhealthy objection to dealing with Rifkind despite the fact he holds all the trump cards. I found it incredible that at the last meeting, one of the executives guilty of failing to secure the Railtrack freehold was allowed to argue the case for doing nothing so that Rifkind could not benefit."

An anonymous MCC employee sent this letter to members following Bradshaw's return to Australia (November 2011):

"It is no secret that since the departure of Keith Bradshaw, there is an atmosphere of fear and suspicion within the club. I am very much in favour of the original 'Vision' for reasons that will become apparent further on.

HOWEVER, I FIRMLY BELIEVE (LIKE YOU) THAT ANY DECISION TAKEN TO ADOPT THE 'VISION,' OR ABORT, MUST BE TAKEN BY ALL THE MEMBERSHIP. FURTHERMORE THIS DECISION CANNOT BE MADE UNTIL ALL THE MEMBERS ARE FULLY AQUAINTED WITH ALL THE FACTS.

The Rifkind Levy Partnership approached Roger Knight in 2004, offering a sum of £50m in exchange for a licence to build residential flats on the leasehold strip above the freehold land owned by RLP. After a couple of brief discussions with Charles Rifkind, Knight and Maurice de Rohan (the then chairman of the estates committee) refused to pursue the matter any further or have any contact.

Soon after Keith Bradshaw's appointment, he agreed to meet with Rifkind and listen to what he had to propose. Keith believed that the offer of substantial sums of money would allow the club to develop the ground in its entirety rather than the piecemeal and random developments that had taken place over the previous 25 years. The first step was to appoint a firm of international architects to create a masterplan for future development. You will no doubt recall the membership being informed of this and asked (in a questionnaire) what their priorities would be. As you know, the world-renowned firm of Herzog & de Meuron were selected and given a brief, disseminated from the members questionnaire.

The so-called change of mind and the disbanding of the development committee was a direct result of the threat by Stocken and Dowley to resign. I understand from another member of the committee it was the nastiest, most vicious meeting he had ever attended. Why did the committee change their minds? Simply because they did not want the public humiliation and press publicity if the chairman and secretary of finance of MCC were to resign.

Yes, Keith made his mind up to resign as a result of this meeting. As you know, Keith's mother sadly died during the Sri Lanka Test and it was on his return from Australia that he agreed with Stocken to announce his resignation for family reasons. This was only partly true and illustrates Keith's honour and loyalty to the club, in that he did not want to 'rock the Boat' and bring the sordid truth into the open.

Almacantar will be suing the club for £750,000 (for fees owing) unless there is a prior mutual settlement. The residential development was the catalyst for the 'Vision.' In the early discussions, Rifkind detailed the square footage he required and the architects incorporated this into the designs for the blocks of flats. It is most important to acknowledge that the roadshow consultations undertaken by David Batts (assistant secretary and chief executive) and attended by some 2,000 members around the country overwhelmingly approved the 'Vision,' the scale model of which clearly included the five blocks of flats. Bearing in mind this fact, it is incredulous for the president to claim in his letter that it was 'the committee's belief that members would not be inclined to accept such a scheme.' So we have the position whereby some 2,000 members are ignored and outvoted by 15 committee members!

The original Herzog de Meuron 'Vision' was as you know thrown out in 2011 in favour of a more modest scheme. At the same time, the committee appointed Savills to re asses the original 'Vision.' How daft can you get?

I would like to suggest the following:

- An enquiry, followed by a special general meeting.

- An sgm is convened to vote upon the original Herzog & de Meuron 'Vision'.

- The proposers and seconders for and against the 'Vision' should NOT be committee members as I believe they would have an unfair advantage and be in a position to instruct the secretariat to withhold vital information from the members.

- I would suggest that Robert Griffiths proposes and John Major seconds the 'Vision.' If Stocken and Dowley wish to oppose it then they should first resign from the committee, or alternatively ordinary members, the likes of Dr Knott and Mr. Holmes, should oppose.

- The chair should be taken by one of the trustees. Certainly not the president, who has already made clear his views.

- Prior to this extraordinary general meeting, ALL details, documents etc. of the 'Vision' from its very inception should be made available to both sets of proposers and seconders. They should then be allowed to convey their views and recommendations to ALL the members of the club in writing.

Only after this process has been completed, should the sgm take place. This may take a year to complete, and cost a lot of money, but in the context of the importance of the 'Vision' for the next 100 years in Lord's, it would be time and money well spent. We all agree this will be the most important decision taken since the move into the current ground in 1814.

In conclusion, the experiences of Robert Griffiths QC, the development committee chairman. are an insight into the defective governance of MCC. His final analysis is revealing:

'There was no good reason for the abandonment of the 'Vision for Lord's' and the disbandment of the development committee comprising an extremely distinguished team of individual talent. It was a totally illogical decision. We had recommended unanimously to the main committee that in difficult circumstances we wished to enter into a period of exclusive negotiations with the developer. Our main purpose was to oversee the submission of the planning application for the delivery of the 'Vision.' The shock termination of such valuable human endeavour and the selfless service given for the benefit of MCC and its members is beyond comparison.'

What is unforgiveable and remains unforgotten is the committee's refusal to accede to the urgent appeal for an independent investigation and their malign opposition to the membership sgm resolution of October 17 2013. An emollient has never been applied to a constantly festering wound whereby the MCC committee suffers from the amnesia of failing to act as an agent and the guardian of the best interests of the membership of MCC. It should never be insulated from the consequences of its perennial abuses of power. Where have the MCC trustees been hiding since the end of World War II? Why did they not oppose their traditional responsibilities of acting in good faith in the Lord's court of appeal on behalf of the MCC membership being removed at the sgm in May 2004? There is no record of any executive trustee decision being determined since the appointment of Glyn Mills as the custodian trustee on August 31 1937. Years of trustee silence!

MCC member rights and privileges amount to nothing more than paying an annual subscription to buy a season ticket to watch cricket at Lord's but with a significant downside – an obligation to finance the annual deficits of the MCC Royal Charter Corporation in perpetuity. The club has become a ponzi scheme of epic proportions, with a 30-year waiting list of people having paid a membership registration fee to join the privileged queue outside the Grace Gates at NW8 8QN. These MCC candidates awaiting election are joined in the queue by an army of debenture shareholders agreeing to wait 75 years for an interest free loan to be redeemed. Such is the power of a world-class heritage site cricket ground in London where an operation of biblical deceit is practised within a Royal Charter Corporation with the patronage of a King.

A true story that should surely feature as the unlikely subject of a novel?"

I have to admit to being unfamiliar at the time with the details of the task that faced Bradshaw when he decided to explore the possibility of property development at Lord's soon after he arrived in 2006 but it could well be that the stress he encountered on the way shortened his life.

*

In 2024 a rare chance to redress these disastrous failures and grasp another significant commercial opportunity arose with the resignation of Lavender, hence vacating an MCC-owned house on Grove End Road. Once again it became possible to envisage a holistic approach to the development of the Lord's estate at the western end. Only personal pride stands in the way.

The continuing doubts over the future of Test match cricket at Lord's and the unknown eventual cost of rebuilding the Tavern and Allen stands adds uncertainty to the wisdom of an ECB-led attempt to introduce franchise cricket at Lord's. It was perhaps unwise of MCC at this early juncture to consider accepting large amounts of money in return for the club's involvement in the monetised sport. Little did I think that the Cowdreys and Dexters in their amateur days would be eclipsed by the professionals today – perhaps better described as mercenaries. I therefore recognise a clear separation of those of us who played and continue to play cricket for the love of it and within the spirit of the game governed by traditional laws from professionals participating in activities that rank as a sport that is better called 'sloggit.' Cricketers turn into family men – and women – and have to make a living. Numerous amateurs, like Cowdrey, who married into money, had private means and hence could be regarded as fortunate. Others, like Trevor Bailey, could continue to play cricket without remuneration through taking on other roles in addition – in his case becoming secretary of Essex. Even Dexter had bills to pay eventually. But would he have wished to have become a freelance bat-for-hire?

Given MCC's principal traditional role as the owner of both the laws of cricket and Lord's cricket ground, it is surely the club's principal duty to retain its independence, free of purely commercial motives, as the guardian and trustee of cricket and in particular the ethics of the amateur game entrenched within grass roots cricket – schools, universities and clubs. MCC must live or die with members being known for 'playing the game' in all walks of life.

In 2025 MCC had an annual turnover close to £68m. Membership subscriptions amount to £8.7m. Yet year-by-year it manages to incur trading losses and still embraces woefully ineffective management and administration. The consequence has been years of prodigal waste and a general lack of accountability that has had lasting negative results both for the club itself and for its 18,000 full members and 5,700 associate members – not to mention all those on a waiting list to join. This stretches out to more than 25 years.

Robert Ebdon denied Charles Rifkind access to Lord's for an organised pre-arranged meeting with the Arbitrator of the Rent Review inspection July 2023 of the Leasehold Land at the Nursery End.

Herzog De Meuron lectern designs of the Compton and Edrich Stands having a roof, unlike the preferred edifices with no roofs

"The MCC committee's too much of a weird, back-scratching chumocracy for my liking."

Chapter 8 – Trustees and a Lack of Trust.
The absence of a Court of Appeal

Chapter 8
Trustees and a Lack of Trust

A letter to me from Guy Lavender, MCC's secretary and chief executive (as the position was now styled) dated August 21 2018 states: "As you will know, this is a matter (the MCC trustees) which you have been discussing with the club for several years, during which time the issues which you raise have been investigated by the club's executive, analysed by several committee members who have enormous legal expertise, as well as external legal advisers to the club. They have all come to the same conclusion – that there is no requirement or need, neither moral nor legal, to pursue any further investigation of this matter (of a trust):

The change of club governance from an unincorporated members association into a Royal Charter Corporation supersedes the past. Having reviewed the documentation, the relevant roles of the trustees and the custodian trustee are explicitly clear, as is the relationship between them."

And so Sir Scott Baker's opinion in his report that the role of the trustees requires a clearer definition is to be dismissed!

As a schoolboy I was taught to use capital letters in connection with words having a particular meaning as opposed to the meaning in general.

The word 'trustee' has been used in the MCC rules since 1867 and more recently in the MCC Royal Charter Article 2 (i) 'Trustee *shall mean those members appointed as such by the MCC committee with such powers and duties (and solely such powers and duties as are provided in the rules and subject to approval of the members in accordance with the rules.'* In my mind therefore the MCC trustees are special people with special duties. However, the word within the club rules remains with an uncertain definition resembling Alice's logical struggle with her words in Wonderland.

And so, this important subject needs to be addressed in some detail, being intimately associated with the origins of Lord's cricket ground itself. The office of trustee was created by the committee on March 26 1864 when five members were appointed in preparation for vesting the new 99-year lease in their ownership prior to the purchase of the Lord's freehold on August 22 1866. The new trustees were declared at the 1865

DATED 30th August 1937.

45213

The Right Honourable Martin Bladen Baron Hawke and others

— and —

The Right Honourable The Earl of Dartmouth G.C.V.O.

Appointment of a New Trustee
— and —
Vesting Declaration.

The trust deed of 1937, which MCC needs to heed

annual meeting to be persons 'whose names are a sufficient guarantee for the future prosperity and welfare of MCC.' They numbered 22 in the years 1865-1945 (80 years) and since then a further 40 trustees (80 years) have been appointed.

Trustees have an implied duty of care – in accordance with the Trustee Acts 1925 and 2000. Duties are to:

- Carry out the expressed terms of the trust instrument (Where is it?)
- Defend the trust (What type – is it express, implied or bare?)
- Prudently invest trust assets (What and where are they listed?)
- Be impartial among the beneficiaries (MCC members)
- Account for actions and keep beneficiaries informed (accountability)
- Be loyal
- Not delegate
- Not profit
- Not have any conflict of interest (club officer or ex-committee member)
- Administer in the best interest of the beneficiaries (MCC members)

The MCC trustees of today fail the litmus test in spectacular fashion on several counts, the most important of all being the conflict of interest famously described by Patrick Milmo QC as the 'Two Hat Syndrome' at Lord's. How can any MCC trustee act in a trustworthy manner having been appointed by the committee as an ex-committee member? The situation, if it was not so serious, is laughable. As recently as the 2023 annual meeting I drew attention to this unacceptable situation and still the trustees remained mute. One would have thought the conduct of the meeting would have been a matter of concern and yet was dismissed by the lawyers present.

Appeals made to the club trustees have always been ignored

or dismissed and only one trustee since World War II has questioned his duties and responsibilities at a committee meeting – John Woodcock in 1996. It took Sir Scott Baker in 2002 to alert the committee to his serious doubts over the duties and responsibilities of the MCC trustees. He observed: "The role of the MCC trustees is unclear and there is a view in some quarters that the method of appointing trustees adds to the perception of a self-perpetuating oligarchy." Hence the propagation of a belief that the letters MCC stand for the Marylebone Chums Club! One would have thought Sir Scott's intervention would have been a siren call to the committee for action, but nothing has been determined since.

If the club was properly incorporated within our Royal Charter and a new governance structure was in place, the role of the trustees would be much easier to define, with Lord's cricket ground being the subject of a limited company registration and managed by a board of directors. However, we are where we are.

In the absence of another definition of the meaning of 'trustee' in the club rules, it is reasonable to assume that the traditional common law meaning still applies. The registered trustee deeds of August 1937 are ample evidence of the Lord's cricket ground trust. Revised rules in 2004 have effectively attempted to create a new class of trustee within the club with few, if any, of the traditional duties of care being apparent. The new use of the term 'trustee' in the club rules is therefore misleading and unlawful. Even the appointment of a custodian trustee is now under the complete control of the committee and despite the MCC Royal Charter status is still featured in the rules.

The rules of 1867 decreed that not more than five and not fewer than three MCC members be appointed trustees for life at any one time. Their authority was to be significant since they were designated principal officers of the club, ex-officio voting members of the committee and enjoying a lifetime appointment.

Any replacement had to be appointed by the remaining trustees who required sight of a death certificate before any new appointment could be made. In effect, they were a 'counsel of wise owls' and a court of appeal charged with the responsibility of ensuring the club was properly governed with continuity. The 1865 agm minutes record the loyal toast being made to HRH the Prince of Wales as patron of MCC and the *'whole property being vested in five trustees whose names are a sufficient guarantee for the future welfare and prosperity of MCC.'*

Soon after World War II the trustee patronage was significantly diluted with the committee deciding their appointment should be for three-year terms. Since that time all the trustees' duties and responsibilities have been gradually stripped away. First came a reduction in their numbers to four in 1951 and to three in 1964, so losing two committee votes. Secondly, they ceased to be principal officers of the club and thirdly, their committee votes were removed and they could only attend committee meetings as observers. Today the trustees are mere eunuchs – all ex-committee members appointed for three to six years, enjoying various committee privileges as part of what has become nothing more than a long-service committee medal award.

Perhaps the greatest and most significant loss, however, is the traditional trustee powers of a final veto of any sale of Lord's and ground development plans. Had the MCC trustees acted in good faith over the 'Vision for Lord's' development plans in 2011 and four years later over the Royal Charter restructuring plans, the club would not be in such a right royal mess today. This raises the question of whether a breach of trust has been executed by the committee in removing the lawful duties of the trustees first endowed in 1866. Matters now are even more complicated through MCC becoming a Royal Charter Company. The surgeons responsible for excising the MCC trustee duties and responsibilities require indictment.

Why did the trustees not intervene in the row over the use

of Lord's by the TCCB in 1987? Why was there no trustee veto exercised to prevent expensive development at Lord's in the absence of any long-term contract for the future use of Lord's by the ECB with a guaranteed income stream to fund the capital investment (member welfare?)

Members may even profit from the sale of Lord's – in direct contravention of the original terms of the purchase of the ground. This reality is enshrined in Article 14 of the Royal Charter. It was made possible by a change in the club rules in the 1970s at a time when the trustees could still veto any member profit from the dissolution of MCC. Since then, the trustee powers of veto have been abolished, preventing members assuming a proprietary interest in the Lord's real estate.

Over the years the MCC committee has closed one door after another to avoid member dissent or dissatisfaction causing any unwelcome change to committee authority. The egregious use of the remote ballot vote has been largely responsible for the death of democracy at Lord's. How can wholesale changes in the rules be validated by fewer than ten per cent of the membership (2022)? Proper scrutiny exercised by the secretary and suitably endowed trustees would never permit the committee to enjoy unfettered power.

Now, even e-mail correspondence raising matters of concern often remains unanswered or unattended. This unhealthy trend began with rule changes designed to remove the ability of members to raise matters for discussion on the ordinary business agenda at an annual meeting. These prohibited a proposer and seconder present to speak to a formal resolution that could be subjected to a binding poll. Instead, to have a resolution passed at an agm or sgm, it is now necessary for 120/180 members to sign requisition forms in advance of a resolution being submitted.

The words of any resolution need to be approved to the "reasonable satisfaction" of the committee and then made the subject of a remote ballot *before* any general meeting has been lawfully convened. Such resolutions are subject also to vetting by the club lawyer and/or an external law firm in order to approve their 'legality' under the rules. Frequently, such resolutions are ruled out of order on obscure technical grounds through this process. Even if they do reach the agm/sgm agenda goal, the use of the remote vote backed by a committee recommendation on how it wishes members to vote will invariably decide the matter against the requisitionists in the absence of any discussion.

The misuse of the remote voting procedures to ward off 'grass roots' initiatives/opposition from members, coupled with the continued erosion of member rights through regular club rule changes, has effectively neutralised all member opposition and democratic government. The manner in which the committee exercises dictatorial powers over the day to day management of affairs at Lord's must end. No court of appeal convened by the MCC trustees should ever permit such an abuse of power.

The Appointment of the Original Trustees and their Duties

At the annual meeting of May 23 1864 the proceedings of the committee were ratified and five founding trustees were appointed for life:

- 1st Earl of Dudley
  d May 7 1885 aged 68. Trustee for 21 years

- 4th Earl of Sefton
  d June 27 1897 aged 61. Trustee for 33 years

- 6th Earl of Bessborough (Hon Frederick Ponsonby)
  d March 11 1895 aged 79. Trustee for 29 years

- RJP Broughton
  d June 15 1911 aged 94. Trustee for 47 years

- WA Nicholson
  d July 25 1909 aged 84. Trustee for 45 years

Broughton (a lawyer) was undoubtedly chosen as a trustee

because of his specialist knowledge of trust law (ref Case Law Broughton v Langley). Being a partner in a London law firm, it is inconceivable that a deed of trust ordered by the MCC committee (March 26 1866) was not prepared and executed at the time.

The Lord's Trust

A public appeal was created to assist with the financing of the purchase of Lord's with a donation fund opened by messrs Drummonds to which HRH the Prince of Wales donated. Messrs Bailey, Shaw, and Bailey of 5, Berners Street were the appointed club solicitors at the time.*

Proposals to purchase the leasehold of Lord's from JH Dark and vesting the 'whole property' in the care of the five MCC trustees were initially suggested at a committee meeting held on April 8 1864 and later approved at a special general meeting at the Freemasons' Tavern on May 3 1865 (club records).

On March 26 1866 the committee ordered 'The five trustees to execute a deed of trust as to Lord's ground being held in trust for MCC' (committee minutes p 491). The Lord's cricket freehold was conveyed into the hands of the trustees on August 22 1866 when the trust formally came into existence (see deed of trustee appointment August 30 1937 first schedule No 1 – appendix A). At the annual meeting May 1 1867 'the trustees were authorised to charge the freehold and leasehold property of the club by way of mortgage for securing the money lately advanced for the purchase of Lord's cricket ground by William Nicholson (1866).' The duty of the trustees was stated to 'guarantee the welfare and prosperity of the club' together with the preservation of the 'whole property' and assets of the club for the benefit of the members and their successors forever (agm minutes dated May 3 1865). Provision was made in the club rules (1866) for a maximum of five and a minimum of three MCC trustees who were appointed for life (rule IX).

In the club rules the trustees were listed as officers of MCC and ex-officio committee members (see agm 1867 minutes) with full powers to overrule the committee via sgm in pursuance of the primacy and guardianship of statutory trust law. Until relatively recently (1983) the trustees retained the power of veto over the disposal of any freehold or leasehold property (Rule X para 46). They also controlled the issue of debentures and ground development.

The deed of trustee appointment dated August 30 1937 (Earl of Dartmouth) confirms the entrenchment of a special duty of care concerning the Lord's Trust. The deed includes reference in the second para '…subject to trusts for the club…' The deed of appointment of the custodian trustee enacted the following day by the five MCC trustees was made, subject to Section 4 sub-sections (2) and (3) of the Public Trustee Act 1906.

MCC Trustee Rule changes

The club rules of 1946 continued to confirm the traditional independent status of the five trustees, but in 1951 their number was reduced to four, most probably in recognition of the Trustee Act 1925 requirements for land being held in trust. Sir Pelham Warner was the last lifetime MCC trustee and upon his retirement in 1962 (ill health) the number of trustees was further reduced to three.

In 1976 the three trustees remained as officers of the club and ex-officio committee members. However, by this time trustee appointments were under the control of the committee and their service reduced to three-year terms of office.

In January 2004 the 'memorandum on the proposed revisions to the rules of the club' contained the following statement: 'Rule 16. The powers and duties of the trustees have been clarified and broadened.' In practice their officer status together with their statutory powers endowed by tradition and Statute Trust Law 1906 was extinguished at the 2004 sgm.

Confirmation of Trust – the evidence

The lawful implications of the committee minute dated March 26 1866 were very clear when the trustees were ordered to execute a deed of trust in preparation for the conveyance of Lord's into their care. The trustees were recorded in the club rules as being officers of the club and ex-officio members of the MCC committee (annual meeting May 1 1867). In accordance with trustee custom and practice at the time they were appointed for life and the surviving MCC trustees appointed their successors only on production of death certificates. A number of death certificates of MCC trustees (9) can be seen in the club archives and a deed of appointment dated August 30 1937 in respect of the Earl of Dartmouth confirms the trustee status under the primacy of statute law.

A deed of conveyance made the following day refers (paras 1 & 2) to section 4 sub sections (2) and (3) of the Public Trustee Act 1906 being applicable in respect of the appointment of the custodian trustee by the managing trustees.

The Implications of the MCC Trustee Rule changes

The implications of the various rule changes, made in respect of the status of the MCC trustees since 1946, are profound. Some conflict with the primacy of statutory trust law. The fact the committee in recent years chooses to appoint ex-committee members without exception as MCC trustees undermines a basic requirement of trustees being free from conflicts of interest. The use of the word 'trustee' endows lawful implications.

As we have seen, at the annual meeting in 1987 the report and accounts were rejected for the first time in the history of the club as a result of the MCC committee granting rights and privileges to the TCCB for the use of Lord's without the consent or approval of the MCC trustees acting on behalf of and in the best interests of the MCC members. The committee actions prejudiced the rights and privileges of MCC members and were in breach of trust.

In the light of the evidence cited it is held that the MCC committee and the MCC trustees are in breach of the Lord's Trust (1866) as a result of rule changes that conflict with statutory trust law. The changes made to the club rules in respect of the lawful status (trustee act) of the MCC trustees ordered by various MCC committees since 1973 (notwithstanding the transfer of powers of appointment and change in period of office) constitute serious breaches of the Lord's Trust (1866). With the recognition of trustees (including a custodian trustee) in the club rules comes the acknowledgement of a trust. Rule XII of 1867 makes the position crystal clear and the committee therefore does not have unfettered powers of management over the club assets held in trust in the absence of formal approval from the trustees acting as guardians of the sovereign rights and privileges of the MCC members. The Lord's trust was established for very good reason – to ensure the best interests of the members are protected at all times by trusted guardians (trustees) whose duties and responsibilities are enshrined in statutory trust law.

The MCC committee have, in recent years, committed serious breaches of trust and been negligent in the guardianship of Lord's" has failed to ensure the club assets have have been employed to the best advantage to *guarantee the welfare and prosperity of the MCC members.*

* Bailey, Shaw and Smith were established in 1836 at 5 Berners Street, London. It became Bailey, Shaw, Smith and Bailey in 1847 and settled on its final title in 1875. It is possible this law firm acted as club solicitors until the death of RJP Broughton (MCC trustee) in 1911. It disappeared with the amalgamation into Speechley, Bircham and Company in 1997 (lately Charles Russell Speechley), having moved from Berners Street in about 1990.

Halsey Lightly followed BSSB as club solicitors for more than 70 years, being replaced by Simmons and Simmons in 1987.

"That's a funny spelling of 'Chairman'."

Chapter 9 – Chairmen and Conundrums
A structural governance problem

Chapter 9
Chairmen and Conundrums

A dispassionate observer will conclude two things about the appointments of MCC chairmen and presidents down the years. In the case of the latter, the election for this titular role is in the gift of the incumbent and world-class cricketing talent denotes clear merit. A different explanation is required for the former, a position that came into being only at the start of the 21st century. And this has hardly been a successful innovation. It could well be said that four of the first seven incumbents – Sir Michael Jenkins, Oliver Stocken, Gerald Corbett and Bruce Carnegie-Brown – were failures. Lord

Bruce Carnegie-Brown former MCC chairman who embarrassed himself at the AGM. Made a sudden departure with an unexpected announcement of not wishing to serve more than one term of 3 years, several days after his profile in the Daily Telegraph

Alexander and Charles Fry, the second and third appointees, were the exception and Mark Nicholas, who came into office in 2024, awaits the judgement of time.

There is an obvious question that arises – is a club chairman necessary or just a job for the boys and girls? We discussed this question at some length in the ISWP report in 2015 and it proved a controversial subject. On balance, however, we concluded this was a 21st century failure. In all but two cases, those of Alexander and Bruce Carnegie–Brown, the incumbents have erred and strayed from the rule book. Their very narrow duty is simply stated as being non-executive. Their duty is to 'act as the chair at meetings of the MCC committee.' Period.

Sir Michael Jenkins, the first chairman of MCC, appeared on the scene as one of the chosen few at Lord's in 1993. He had joined the Foreign Office in 1959, having read French and Russian at Cambridge and completed his diplomatic service as ambassador to the Netherlands in 1988. His interest in Russian affairs and a posting to Moscow encouraged him to publish his book *Arakcheyev – Grand Vizier of the Russian E*mpire, his father having sparked an interest in his becoming a scholar of Byzantine history. He decided upon a change of career and became deputy chairman of Dresdner Kleinwort Bank and six years later was appointed president of Boeing (UK). He joined MCC's members and general purposes sub-committee in 1993, all of which prepared him for his planned influence in MCC affairs.

His rise to greater things at Lord's began with his appointment in 1999 as treasurer.

In January 2000 a 16-page document appeared out of the blue entitled *MCC – Preparing for the Future.* This arrived as a surprise. Being a member of the 1999 president's members liaison group and the staging agreement WP, I would have expected some prior knowledge, but this new high-level initiative had been cloaked in secrecy.

Sir Michael was supported by a very small and select group

– Fry, Philip Hodson, Stocken, Anthony Wreford and MCC's then secretary, Roger Knight. The back page published six members' informal discussion meeting dates in early April at Lord's and four other venues. Attendees had to book in advance and were limited to 100 members attending each ground. There was to be no voting at these informal regional meetings at Lord's (x 2) Trent Bridge, Bristol, Old Trafford and Edgbaston. Plans were in place to implement the necessary rule changes at the special general meeting on May 3 2000.

The document stated: 'Striving to maintain equilibrium between the conflicting needs of MCC as a private member club and its public role in the maintenance and development of cricket are the main objectives to justify the outside world's perception of MCC as the finest cricket club in the world.'

There is no mention of any ground development and it continued: 'It is clear that there are no major developments and challenges to the club in almost every aspect of its operations. MCC has a management structure that has remained largely unchanged for nearly 30 years. However appropriate this may have been in the past it is increasingly apparent that the club needs restructuring in order to operate efficiently and effectively in the current environment and to be prepared for the challenges of the near future.' The 30 years is much more like 130 years as the committee has been responsible for the entire management of club affairs ever since 1866 when Lord's was bought.

The Jenkins document was given the task of devising a new management structure that would be clear and understandable to all concerned. It needed to be unambiguous as to the responsibilities of the executive staff and the non-executives whilst rationalising and simplifying the club management and including an appropriate system of checks and balances. There was to be a newly appointed executive board with delegated powers, a club chairman/treasurer, a newly styled secretary and chief executive and a deputy chief executive. The membership and general purposes committee was retitled the 'membership committee.' Eight sub-committees were to be reduced to five. In conclusion 'the committee believes the changes will bring about significant improvements in the club's management' but there was nothing about the management of the Lord's estate itself.

The committee agreed to review the effectiveness of the new system in October 2001. Meanwhile, the rule changes were on the business agenda for the annual meeting of 2000 and Sir Michael's team agreed he should be the first chairman/treasurer in the history of MCC with the secretary appointed as chief executive. Only a few weeks beforehand my patience had been severely tested by the secretary's inefficiency. There was some sense behind the decision to end the office of treasurer as there was also a chairman of finance appointment (Oliver Stocken) with his deputy (Justin Dowley). These did cause some debate at the time as both had been prominent contributors to the discussions concerning the failed Railtrack auction bid.

The independence of the club is always deemed to be precious and maintaining Lord's as a world-class cricket ground is another imperative. But there was a lack of real substance in the document and not much more than painters and decorators being employed to paper over the ever more obvious cracks in the committee room plaster. There was no attempt whatsoever to consider a separation of powers to manage the membership (administration and the secretariat) and Lord's property (commercial and a board of executive directors). The stark failure in the commercial management of Lord's cricket ground as the club's main profit centre was made clear in the special working party report of 1984. It remains the same today with the committee suffering from tunnel vision on property development.

It is noticeable how the cricketer club of old has gradually metamorphosed into the cricket club of today. The transition from running and financing international cricket matches both here and abroad brought unseen difficulties for the club in the early 1970's and not until 1987 did the full extent of the problems surface.

Jenkins joined two other MCC principal officers in 2000: Lord Alexander (president) as well as being chairman of National Westminster Bank; and Stocken (treasurer) who was financial director at Barclay's Bank. All three were non-cricketers; there had been rumblings about too many well-known cricketers being elected to the main committee. A lack of 'skill sets' was offered as an excuse for starring favoured candidates at election time. The annual report of 2000 discloses Nicholas, the former Hampshire captain, arriving on the committee scene as an elected member. The report reduced the number of sub-committees from eight to five: cricket, estates, finance, marketing and membership. Other elected committee members included Jack Bailey and John Stephenson, two retired MCC secretaries.

My unhappiness was expressed to Jenkins in a number of e-mail exchanges and at a difficult meeting with him at his London HQ of Dresdner Bank where we sat at opposite ends of a huge committee room table – in the style of President Putin of Russia many years later (not a cricketer so far as we know). I was reminded of this meeting when a picture of him appeared sitting at the head of a table many metres long during the Covid crisis to distance himself at meetings from possible infection. Perhaps Sir Michael considered me to pose a similar risk as a leper.

I found it odd that nowhere in his document did he mention member rights and privileges and the benefits of an elected membership committee. A democratic deficit was the subject of an attractive remedy in our ISWP report of 2015, only to be trashed by the new chairman, Gerald Corbett, who set his hand against what he called an elected 'second chamber' with powers to challenge the main committee. Exactly the reason for our proposal!

By a strange coincidence we had debated that the position of chairman was an unnecessary appendage.

Jenkins defined the new chairman's role as having a non-executive function. However, there is strong evidence of five successive chairmen having had a very strong influence on executive functions. Charles Fry, Alexander's successor, was perhaps the most anodyne, although he was a very keen supporter of the club's secretary and chief executive, Keith Bradshaw, as any good chairman should have been. Stocken who succeeded Fry prematurely, and Corbett, the next in line, stand out as the most controversial, in my opnion. I have experienced personally the significant effect that the chairman can have on influencing a committee decision in giving not just a steer but a directive. In the instance of resisting the 'Vision for Lord's' in 2011 the committee should have accepted the resignations of both Stocken and Dowley as chairman and treasurer as they are responsible for the schism that still exists today.

In my experience of corporate matters, the chairman should be considered a wise owl to be consulted in times of need and kept away from tinkering with the levers of executive power. In the incident of the demise of 'the Vison,' matters were made far worse by the fact the club trustees were no longer committee members. If ever there was an occasion that needed trustee intervention, this was it. If the trustees had retained their powers of 1999 the lack of confidence in Bradshaw, 12 years later, could never have occurred.

What is particularly puzzling is that Stocken put his name to the Sir Scott Baker SWP and yet failed later as chairman. He had endorsed the belief that MCC "is the owner of the finest cricket ground in the world and MCC should not only maintain and develop Lord's as a world-class ground but also seek to improve facilities." How can his subsequent executive actions, that halted this vision in its tracks, be reasonable? With his commercial background at Barclay's Bank, he was well placed to oversee the much-needed structural re-organisation and transforming an unincorporated cricket club owning a large property portfolio.

Moving on, Stocken was responsible for grasping the

incorporation nettle in appointing an Incorporation WP in April 2011 whilst the ground development row was still simmering. I think he recognised the advantages incorporation would bring and the future of Lord's cricket ground being secured. However, in March 2015 at a Structure WP meeting, the deputy secretary, Colin Maynard, launched a missile that struck at the heart of our recommendations. From nowhere, he produced a very scruffy 11-page booklet he had prepared with RLP (Rifkind Levy Partnership featuring large; after Jonathan Levy' retirement, Charles Rifkind was the sole director) appearing in very heavy typescript within five of the first six pages. What was going on?

This was a harbinger of things to come and the appearance of Shakespeare's "treasons, stratagems and spoils" to wreck two and a half years of work planning the restructuring of MCC. Our final ISWP report was never circulated to members for discussion; many will have never seen it. For some unknown reason Stocken failed to honour his promise of circulating his WP report as a consultative green paper and he allowed Corbett to direct the committee to trash it. The president, David Morgan, took the unusual step of sending a letter to us. This in effect read "Thank you – goodbye."

My personal communications expressing concerns are recorded shortly before the musical chairs began in 2000 with Jenkins, whose new career was demanding too much of his time and attention, resigning as MCC chairman after only one year in office.

> To: Sir Michael Jenkins
> From: Nigel Knott
> Fax:
> Date: 26/02/2000
> cc Robert Griffiths Esq. QC
>
> Dear Sir Michael,
>   I am sorry that we have not been able to speak on the telephone and hope that we will have done so by the

time this reaches you. It is perhaps a good thing that you should have hard copy anyway.

You will be in the chair at the first executive meeting on Tuesday and I trust that this initiative will have greater success than the last attempt to institute an executive committee in 1989. On your agenda will be discussion about the Lord's website on which I have already given my views to you by e-mail. I am anxious that you should be fully briefed as I do not believe that the complete picture has been revealed to you yet. Indeed, it has brought to my attention (the matter is too sensitive to disclose here) that the whole staging working party initiative and the efforts of Robert Griffiths were this week in danger of being undermined (I think that sabotaged would be a better word) by members of the committee. All our hard work and considerable patience were on the brink of being destroyed by the personal agendas of at least two committee members. I am frankly shocked but in the light of my detailed knowledge of affairs within the club in the past not altogether surprised.

This latest failure of the committee to support Tony Lewis' members liason group (mlp) initiative and the suppression of much of the discussion from the membership. All sorts of platitudes and excuses have been made but the lack of communication is unacceptable. So is the lack of communication from the staging working party after more than 18 months hard work. I have conveyed a considerable amount of information to Tony Lewis about my unhappiness but get the feeling that he is not receiving the necessary support either – indeed I detect an element of tiredness in his attempt to redress the various conflicts of interest. Under normal conditions all of this would have been dealt with by an efficient club secretary but my last attempt to talk with him (Roger Knight) was greeted with the comment "Nigel, I am extremely busy and really do not have the time to talk with you as I must get on with other matters." I find his patronising attitude deeply offensive and guaranteed to lead to trouble. As you may know he has already refused to talk with members about other sensitive affairs which he considers is "holding up the carrying on of normal club business."

I must return to the main reason for my communication. The staging working party has worked hard to return to MCC our independence at Lord's and wrest from the ECB the burgeoning oppression that they exercise over us and the other Test match grounds (TMG) to the extent that our financial affairs have been seriously affected. Robert Griffiths has worked selflessly to ensure that in particular the valuable digital electronic transmission rights over and above the conventional forms of broadcasting have been reserved. We have always been aware of the huge potential value of these rights but in view of the extraordinary stock market interest in these activities, unable to value them with any accuracy. It is becoming very obvious that we do in fact own at Lord's the 'pot of gold' which I have believed to exist for some considerable time. Indeed, confidential discussions with a world-class IT company which specialises in interactive TV and internet development has revealed an initiative which has the potential to create at Lord's a £1billion company in five years as an internet services provider. If this is taken on board as a TMG initiative headed up by MCC and supported by MCC then the figures could be doubled. This initiative is of truly breathtaking proportions and one of the most exciting developments to have arrived on our doorstep in the 35 years that I have been a member of MCC. And yet last Tuesday an attempt was made to torpedo the whole initiative.

Sir Michael, we need to speak urgently and in any event before Tuesday next.

Best wishes,
Nigel.

And again to Jenkins on 31/3/2000, having got nowhere:

Dear Sir Michael,

I find the behaviour at Lord's quite extraordinary – the policy of a wilful silence being entertained even more puzzling. I have appealed to you and the president of my club in the capacity as the two senior officers to address some pretty serious issues. What is the reaction – one of concern and the offer to carry out an immediate investigation? No, it is one of anger and annoyance, a breach of trust with the release of confidential correspondence, the diktat by the secretary that I should not be spoken to and a scurrying round to the lawyers to investigate the possibility of a legal action against me (and yet more extortionate legal bills which have to be paid by the members). There is a steadfast refusal to discuss anything associated with the past, just in case the future agendas end in disarray. Perhaps Dennis Silk should have named me personally as an enemy of the club. Perhaps I am seen as a naughty schoolboy who should be treated as such? Perhaps I should even be expelled? I await to hear with bated breath the criminal charges which are being prepared! You seem to have got it hopelessly wrong, Sir Michael, and I regret to say that you are in danger of losing respect and credibility.

My motives are pure and simple. It is not that I ask you to judge between shades of grey. You are being asked to decide upon the difference between black and white -the difference between right and wrong. My letter to the secretary of the club contained some serious charges which cannot remain unanswered. Will you as the senior officer of my club please investigate or do I have to resort to other means? If for some reason you are unable to give satisfactory answers, then why can you not have the good manners to tell me so? It seems to not have occurred to some of you on the committee that I have to still discharge my duty as a member of the staging working party (SWP) set up incidentally on my initiative with Alan Meyer, who, let us not forget, was sacked as the club solicitor for refusing to endorse the 1987 annual report and accounts because they contained a false statement made to the club membership. What am I to make of the statement contained in the president's letter and in the club document 'Preparing for the Future.'

Agreement has been reached with the ECB and a fine result achieved? At the time of writing, no staging agreement has been signed and therefore no contract at law exists. This is a clear case of misrepresentation and a contempt for those of us appointed to look after this most sensitive of issues. Here, again, in my opinion, there is a total failure to keep us properly informed. Misleading statements should have been approved first by the SWP. As a member of this SWP I wish to distance myself from these statements and express my disgust over the way in which the affairs appertaining to the SWP are being mishandled. The matter of the internet also remains an issue closely associated with this SWP.

Although the secretary has treated this as a separate issue and arbitrarily decided to take matters into his own hands, I have seen and studied the documents which identify an extra revenue stream well in excess of £1billion for MCC. Why was SWP not kept formally abreast of these matters? The interference in our affairs is intolerable and a tragic lost opportunity. It is of course the same old story of irreconcilable conflicts of interest at Lord's. I have taken careful note of the statement in 'Preparing for the Future' that 'it is essential that everything we do should be soundly based and professionally managed' where the website is concerned. So far, Sir Michael, this whole issue has been associated with bungling ineptitude for which the secretary must shoulder a fair share of blame.

I beseech you to treat this appeal to you with some sense of gravity. It is my earnest belief that a committee of enquiry is now required to investigate this shameful period in our history which started to blacken the sky at Lord's in 1983. It would be nice to think that if this were to happen and the people appointed were to carry the respect and trust of the MCC members there would be some hope for us all. It was my misplaced belief the president's bold initiative appointing the members liason group would be able to achieve this goal, but here again I feel that I have been used and deceived. Why were all our minutes 'confidential?' Where is the report of our meetings? It has not escaped my notice the committee now intends to operate in secret with a proposed rule change at 19.3.

I can only say this behaviour brings Shakespeare's words to mind:

> *O! that estates, degrees, and offices*
> *Were not deriv'd corruptly, and that clear honour*
> *Were purchased by the merit of the wearer.*
> *How many then should cover that stand bare;*
> *How many be commanded that command;*
> *How much low peasantry would then be glean'd*
> *From the true seed of honour; and how much honour*
> *Pick'd from the chaff and ruin of the times*
> *To be new varnish'd!*

Yours sincerely,
Nigel Knott

The day before the 2000 agm I sent Sir Michael another 'reminder':

From: Nigel Knott Subject: MCC

Dear Sir Michael,

I am aware that you are pre-occupied with bank affairs, however, there are serious matters that require a speedy resolution. You will soon become the senior officer of the club and I am entitled to satisfactory answers – particularly over the matter of fraud, breaches of the club rules by the committee and matters relating to special working parties to which I belong. Both the president and secretary have failed to address my concerns – the president passed the matter of fraud to the secretary to investigate. This is rather odd as the secretary failed to take the necessary action when he was informed about it many months ago.

It is some while now since I notified the president of fraud taking place in the Lord's shop. The cricket ball affair may only be part of the problem. I am stunned by the casual way in which this whole matter is being addressed. The secretary, Roger Knight, had the matter brought to his attention on at least two occasions after he returned from compassionate leave in the summer of last year. There was clear evidence of fraud and yet nothing was done. Anyone who has played a reasonable standard of cricket can see that there is something amiss with the product being sold in the Lord's shop. The fact that these balls were made in Pakistan and were stamped 'Marylebone Official Ball Conforming to MCC Regulations made in England' continued to be sold amounts to the fact that those who knew about the matter last year are complicit in the crime. The following points need to be emphasised:

a) The 'Marylebone' was the subject of an investigation and a specialist report was prepared several months ago. The ball is not made in England. Several issues arise from this –

(i) where is the letter of authority which gives permission for the Lord's brand to be used?
(ii) who is responsible for verifying the quality of the balls?
(iii) who commissioned the order and why was this source chosen?
(iv) why are the balls stamped with a grade 1 marking when this gives a clear implication that they comply with BSI 5993?
(v) why are no balls of English manufacture stocked?
(vi) why was a ten-year supply ordered?

You have only to look at the markings to see that it is as plain as a pikestaff that something is wrong. There is plenty more evidence available to confirm that a fraud was taking place last year and allegedly the secretary knew about it. Please tell me, Sir Michael, why Roger Knight has not been suspended and furthermore why he has now been made chief executive? This is only one of a series of issues which should disqualify him from office – you have a copy of my letter to him requesting that he should resign and the supporting evidence.

I should not have to add further fuel to the glowing fire. The finances of the Lord's shop are in a terrible mess. No overheads are included in the agm account figures for the shop, which is operating at a loss. This needs some explanation.

It has been brought to my notice that a £10,000 'introductory fee' is being asked of manufacturers before the Lord's shop will stock their goods. One manufacturer has already paid – where has this money gone and who has approved these payments?

Many other manufacturers have refused to pay what they considered to be a ransom and this accounts for the fact that not a single helmet has been on sale during the busiest time of the season. I understand that the marketing manager in the shop has refused to sign a valid contract of employment. Why is he allowed to work for the club without one? There are many other irregularities. I wish to stress that it is the secretary of the club, the chairman of the marketing sub-committee and the head of marketing who are responsible for these matters – have you yourself, as treasurer, investigated? How can this saga have been allowed to run for so long?

Breaches of Club Rules
You were sent a letter by my solicitors on Friday following a meeting with counsel and I trust that you will take the necessary action swiftly and decisively.

Special Working Parties
This was addressed in my fax which you received on April 12. You have failed to answer any of my concerns.

I trust that you will treat these matters with the gravity that they merit – I can be contacted through my solicitor at any time. It is imperative that you act before these matters deteriorate into a much more serious state of affairs.

Yours sincerely, Nigel J Knott

NB The cricket ball affair reached the front page of the *Sunday Telegraph* following my contact with Westminster trading standards and the Metropolitan Police CID. Lord Alexander informed the police soon after; he would prefer to carry out an internal investigation led by Sir Michael Pickard. Later, the manager of the Lord's shop was sacked.

Lord Alexander, having followed Sir Michael's short spell as chairman, was very much 'hands off' in keeping with the club rules of being restricted to chairing committee meetings. He retired after one three-year term to make way for Charles Fry, who had already announced he was keen to incorporate MCC to remove any member liabilities. For some unknown reason he failed to take the necessary initiative.

Fry had supported Bradshaw's appointment in 2006 and the two together set out plans to develop Lord's in partnership with Charles Rifkind, setting the scene for a future train crash.

Definition of a Corporation

1. A corporation is a legal entity created by individuals, stockholders, or shareholders, with the purpose of operating for profit.
2. Ownership: A corporation is owned by shareholders who hold shares in the company, while a company is typically owned by individuals or partners.
3. Legal Entity: A corporation is considered a separate legal entity from its owners, providing limited liability protection to shareholders. On the other hand, a company is not a separate legal entity, and its owners have unlimited liability.
4. Liability: Shareholders of a corporation have limited liability, meaning their personal assets are protected in case of business debts or lawsuits. In a company, owners have unlimited liability, risking personal assets in case of financial obligations.
5. Formation: Creating a corporation involves formal registration and compliance with specific corporate laws and regulations. In contrast, a company can be formed without strict formalities, often requiring only a business registration.

6. Management: Corporations have a board of directors appointed by shareholders to oversee the company's operations. In a company, management is usually handled by the owners themselves or a designated person.
7. Size: Corporations are typically larger in size, with multiple layers of hierarchy and extensive operations. Companies, on the other hand, can range from small-scale ventures to larger organizations.
8. Public Listing: Corporations have the option to become publicly traded entities by listing their shares on stock exchanges. Companies, by default, are not publicly traded and operate privately.
9. Governance: Corporations are governed by specific corporate laws and regulations, ensuring compliance and transparency. Companies, on the other hand, are governed by partnership or proprietorship laws, which may be less stringent.
10. Taxation: Corporations are subject to corporate taxes, which are often different from individual or partnership tax laws. Companies are typically taxed based on individual or partnership tax laws, depending on their structure.
11. Continuity: Corporations have continuity even after the death of shareholders, as the ownership of shares can be transferred. Companies, especially proprietorships or partnerships, may dissolve upon the death of owners, unless specific arrangements are made.

"You have a problem with your foresight."

Chapter – 10 A Vision Failure
Amaurosis Fugax

Chapter 10
A Vision Failure

The arrival of Gerald Corbett to replace Oliver Stocken as MCC chairman in October 2015 left me in no doubt we were about to experience a six-year term of executive chairman dictatorship. I had clashed with him whilst serving on the ISWP in March 2015. In his term of office he was, allegedly, the cause of the departure of Derek Brewer, Keith Bradshaw's successor as MCC secretary and chief executive. The chairman of ISWP, Peter Leaver QC, told me after an unpleasant row at our March 2015 meeting that he had made a big mistake in supporting his appointment as MCC chairman. I have to say he has proved to be right. A trustee of the club also disclosed to me his concerns over the appointment of someone so autocratic.

Although he was a controversial figure in his time running Railtrack and was widely criticised by passengers for chaos in the early days of privatisation and a fatal train crash at Hatfield, Corbett became chairman of Betfair, the gambling firm, and several other plc's.

Complaints about him and others proved utterly fruitless with MCC's trustees, chief executive and company secretary all remaining silent. Matters were made far worse with the introduction of a nominations committee to remedy an apparent 'skillsets' deficiency with far too many sub-committee volunteers being involved in club affairs as quasi-executives.

Here are details of my dealings with Corbett after he became chairman of MCC:

January 7 2016 08:14:04 GMT
Subject: MCC/ISWP

Dear Gerald,

There is much at MCC that needs addressing as a matter of urgency and the ISWP ideas concerning the creation of a new charitable trust is of great importance. It is not my intention to allow the shortcomings of MCC Foundation to pass unnoticed by the charity commissioners in the absence of any movement here.

Yes, jaw-jaw may be the best route to take but with one condition - an earnest and sincere wish by all parties to plan the way ahead to begin the implementation of the uncontroversial parts of our ISWP report. For you to say the committee and the executive do not agree with our recommendations is just not true. The evidence is there for all to see.

I would welcome a positive response from you and if this is forthcoming perhaps I could invite Gerard Elias to accompany me at our meeting?

I hope you are enjoying the cricket.
As ever,
Nigel

Then on June 10 2020

Dear Gerald,
Reference MCC 2020 annual general meeting report and a/c's

I am writing to you as the non-executive MCC chairman mandated with the responsibility of ensuring all business matters decided at MCC committee meetings are lawful and obey the club rules.

The arrangements being made for the 2020 agm are in breach of the traditional agenda procedures being restricted to the ordinary business of the club. The agm 'explanatory notes' make it very clear the traditional agm arrangements are not possible in the present circumstances. Therefore, the committee has put in place alternative plans to ensure the ordinary business agenda executed at agm is determined with temporary arrangements being in place to allow members to 'exercise their fundamental right of voting on business at the agm' and no other extraordinary or special business must be determined at this agm. Period.

There are two separate matters to consider: a) the arrangements to hold an emergency 'virtual agm' and b) the ordinary business agenda items and the method of determination. It is the nature of the 'business' being proposed at this virtual agm and the emergency measures being employed that invite sanction.

Postal voting was introduced in 1999 for all ordinary business items on the agm agenda for the first time in club history. This year the committee is allowing additional online voting to take place within a window of 4 hours and 29 minutes following the virtual agm to allow member access to the agm proceedings before voting online. This online voting population therefore will be better informed and the two sets of voting patterns (offline/online) will differ.

There are however, two extraordinary business items: 8) life membership and 9) governance, that fall foul of the law as they cannot by any stretch of the imagination be classed as ordinary business items. These are matters of special or extraordinary interest to all MCC members that must necessarily be the subject of special or extraordinary general meeting arrangements called in the traditional manner with a quorum of 50 members being present. The complex rule changes required to implement these extraordinary resolutions require widespread member consultation in advance of formal approval by a special majority at sgm. It is interesting to note the club rules of 1867 (Rule XV111) state only votes cast at sgm by those members actually present at any sgm are valid. This rule remained in principle until 2000.

Your highly contentious personal letter addressed to me dated 23 May 2020 breaches club rule 9 as you have trespassed within the rightful domain of the secretary MCC and seek to influence the outcome of agm agenda items 8) and 9) that must be expunged from the 2020 agm agenda being unlawfully included as ordinary business items. Both resolutions should await formal egm/sgm determination by members in less stressful times via offline methods. By your latest actions you have failed in your duty of care as the chairman of MCC committee meetings to guide the committee in a direction that is in the best interests of the club and all its members.

Finally, a point of order under what should be agenda item 2) 'Matters arising from the 2019 minutes' (Ref agm report p 59 paragraph 5). Mr. JB Mitchell (a lawyer) raised questions concerning the Royal Charter incorporation and the status of Lord's cricket ground. They remain unanswered and furthermore the proposed new rule 19 retains the unnecessary appointment of a custodian trustee seven years after Royal Charter incorporation took place!

I trust you will respond constructively to my objections. Failing this I will join with other MCC members in calling an urgent sgm to address matters.

Sincerely,
Nigel J Knott

Yet on July 6 2023 Corbett posted this comment on MCC's independent on line pavilion (forum):

"I would like to apologise to Robin (Knight), Nigel

Knott, Peter Leaver and the others who served on the ISWP. As I reflect with the benefit of time, they worked hard and diligently in the expectation that what they recommended would be implemented, and it wasn't. The ending was peremptory and I should have handled it better. I regret that and the bad feeling that caused. They have all served the club well, over many years, and deserve our respect and gratitude. Much of what they did was implemented, and the spirit of governance reform lives on. The debate continues as will reform, and all of that is their legacy.

I hope they continue to argue their case and keep governance and change high up on the agenda'

Gerald

And then to me on August 1 2023

Thanks for your emails.

I'm getting good feedback (on the whole!) for my participation on MCCOLP from members of the committee, the executive and other posters. Apparently it's helpful to have the perspective of someone who's sat in the hot seat, as we all see things from the ends of different telescopes. I enjoy participating as the issues will always be important to me and it beats doing sudoku or the crossword.

For obvious reasons I don't want to make things difficult for my successors - these roles are hard enough as it is and I try to make my posts helpful to their cause rather than obstructive. When next in Wiltshire I would love to drop in and see the lion in his lair, but in general think it better to keep to the ground rules I have set myself

Best wishes
Gerald

As to other matters when he took over the chairmanship, Corbett had been quick to pay tribute to the outgoing chairman: "Oliver Stocken leaves the club in good shape, for which he must take credit." Was he just being diplomatic or did he take into account the 'Vision for Lord's' fiasco? Stocken had refused even to allow talks with Charles Rifkind and there was increasing bitterness among dissident members about the dominance of what they saw as a Stocken-led cabal. This was compounded in a vote for four committee vacancies when four preferred choices were 'starred' on the ballot papers, and all prevailed. However, Stocken lost control of the process for his succession after serving his maximum six-year term and Corbett, who applied himself rather than being tapped up, fended off about 30 candidates to be recommended by a nomination panel and then ratified.

It may not be common knowledge that Corbett, allegedly,

Jim Johnston, chairman of MCC's estates committee, who offered Charles Rifkind a £1 increase in the rent review. The arbitrator awarding a significant increase in the review with costs awarded against MCC

was pushed from Railtrack as, according to the *Financial Times*, John Prescott at the Department of Transport had found him a very difficult person to deal with. His cricket credentials are sparse ("I was a good prep school leg-spinner. From there it was all downhill") but he does love watching the game: he came to Lord's on his 12th birthday to see the inaugural county one-day final in 1963 – three years before I played at Lord's. Above all, he was seen as a fresh face with no ties to MCC's recent history.

Relations between the club and Rifkind seemed then to have been repaired. There was a new, far more modest redevelopment plan to build potentially lucrative flats above the tunnels at the Nursery End (the original 'Vision' now long dead) that could fund the rebuilding plan. The club awaited replies to a long list of questions. One issue was whether the flats would obscure the view of the trees behind — which were seen by Gubby Allen as a crucial part of Lord's faux-rural ambience.

MCC, at this juncture, was planning to pay for any redevelopment from its own funds in order to deny Rifkind any additional benefit to his ground rent he received for the club placing the temporary Nursery pavilion above the tunnels. Work began on the first phase of new ground development, the demolition and replacement of the 57-year-old Warner Stand next to the pavilion. The question of how the rest of the work was to be funded to maintain the ground's pre-eminence split the club. Corbett decided a review was in order, putting the alternatives to the membership, having a debate and then coming to a conclusion, all of which would, he believed, make the club a happier place.

Gerald was replaced by Bruce Carnegie-Brown in 2021. He was chairman of Lloyd's of London and Banco Santander, having spent his early days working at Bank of America. At his first MCC agm he managed to insult members suffering the after-effects of gastro-intestinal surgery and afflicted with colostomy bags. He announced the interval break and failed to ensure the microphones had been silenced before making a gob-stopping remark worthy of expulsion. "It is taking them an age to empty their colostomy bags," he said to the treasurer, who was sitting next to him on the top table, which presumably was intended to be a joke. The proceedings were being transmitted online and his comment was picked up by the wife of one of the afflicted members who was attending the meeting.

Carnegie-Brown maintained a low profile after that and I decided to offer him some advice:

Dear Mr. Carnegie-Brown,

I refer you to the copy of my e-mail sent last Wednesday, concerning the unlawful conduct of the procedural matters determined at the MCC agm of May 3 2023. You, as the club chairman, have a duty of care together with the club law officer, Holly Roper-Curzon and the MCC committee, to ensure all matters arising at MCC agms are governed by the rule of law and natural justice. I should not have to remind you that all MCC members are entitled to be treated at all times at Lord's as natural persons and under the protection of the rule of law.

The particular matter in question concerns the fact the 2023 MCC regulations at Part VII (a) publish the following statement: 'The MCC committee may use, both postal and online voting in relation to any resolution, business or subject to be proposed at any general meeting if it considers the resolution, business or subject to be of sufficient importance ......' There is no definition of either 'business' or 'subject' nor have members approved at any time an extension of the club rules to include 'business or subject' matters in remote voting arrangements and in particular at any agm.

The explanatory notes of the 2023 agm state 'all items of business on the agenda are of sufficient importance to justify the use of online and postal voting....' There are 11 agenda items, only two of which at items 7 (a) and (b) are proper resolutions. It seems therefore that the 2023 agm proceedings have all the hallmarks of an extraordinary general meeting and certainly do not include the basic legal requirements of a lawful traditional agm of a Royal Charter Corporation.

This matter is even more significant when the result of the remote voting numbers may have determined the result of all agenda items before the 236th MCC agm had been lawfully convened @15:00hrs on Wednesday May 3 2023. It seems therefore that all agenda items may have no lawful basis to be determined by remote voting arrangements and are ultra vires.

I should also add the 'hybrid' 235th agm in 2022 failed to record the number of votes cast by MCC members in attendance. Company law usually demands a majority of 75 per cent to validate any special resolution from those present and proxy votes cast for any business item such as an increase in member subscriptions. In this case the agenda business item was 'approved' by 1,152 member votes (73.56 per cent) or 6.3 per cent of the 315 eligible members! Is this democracy operating within a Royal Charter Corporation?

As I have requested, please ensure as chairman MCC I am sent an analogue copy of the 2023 agm minutes and you initiate a full enquiry into the conduct of this year's agm, preferably by a suitably qualified KC who is a not an MCC member.

Thank you.
Sincerely,
Nigel Knott (Dr.)
Elected playing MCC member 1966

He had the courtesy to reply to my letter, his precis amounting to "Everything in the Harris Garden at Lord's is lovely and I have no need to worry!"

E-Mail sent before Christmas 2023

Dear Mr. Carnegie-Brown,

Mahdi Choudhury and Alex Boardman have informed me that the club management is now on holiday until January 3 2024 and therefore I am left with no choice but to seek your support urgently, in your capacity as chairman MCC. My reason is to bring to your attention yet another case of a clear breach of the MCC club rules.

Rule 23.1 'Submission of Resolutions' is very clear in the lawful process required for the requisition of an sgm and refers to 'The written requisition may be contained in several form or forms each signed by one or more requisitionists.' The secretary has not only failed to supply the requisitionists with the necessary 'form or forms' in compliance with 23.1 (i) but also I have been informed as a co-signatory of the sgm resolution in question, that the committee has approved our resolution to their 'reasonable satisfaction' in accordance with Rule 23.1 (iii). Now the MCC executive has taken the unusual step in their own interpretation of Rule 23.1 and decided for some unknown reason to introduce an unauthorized and unsafe electronic voting procedure instead.

To make matters worse the online software being purchased by MCC from a company domiciled in the USA is outside the jurisdiction of the UK's information commissioner and GDPR. MCC members will have no knowledge of the cybercrime dangers of submitting their personal signatures electronically to a company domiciled outside the EU. Neither MCC nor the company domiciled in USA has ISO 27001 certification and members cannot be assured the online voting procedure is suitably immunized against cybercrime. This unlawful online voting process should be proscribed immediately for use in this or any other sgm requisition and MCC members warned of the dangers.

Please institute an immediate investigation into this flagrant breach of club rules that introduces an unnecessary risk to the integrity of members' personal data. I assume the club solicitor is the data protection officer who has informed me of an unwillingness to accept instructions from MCC members! If this matter cannot be resolved before January 3 2024 I will refer to the members' reform group and add the names of two more assistant secretaries in a no-confidence vote at sgm. My club is now a Royal Charter Corporation where the rule of law, democratic governance and the preservation of member rights and privileges are sovereign. We as MCC members expect nothing less.

Thank you,
Sincerely,
Nigel Knott (Dr.)

Nothing constructive except for a polite acknowledgement was received.

Dear Mr. Carnegie–Brown,
Re- MCC sgm March 4 2024

I wish to bring to your attention the recent sgm vote over the lack of democracy in the club being fatally flawed and unlawful. A stubborn refusal to address an obvious democratic deficit within the club rules is a precious opportunity lost to address the problem.

It is important for the sake of good order to make it clear at the outset the MCC committee is the appointed agent for the membership and has to exercise a duty of care to act in the best interests of all members at all times. Being a Royal Charter Corporation, MCC members are natural persons entitled to the protection of the rule of law. The MCC committee government should encapsulate the fundamental principles of democracy. It does not.

A) Breaches of the Club Rules and Regulations

1. You as chairman are in breach of Rule 9.2 that clearly states your sole duty is to chair committee meetings. You have strayed from your restrictive brief into an unlawful executive role. The committee member chosen to address the sgm defined your imaginative duties as being "highly complex requiring many difficult skills, to lead the club from within and the ability to manage stakeholders and represent MCC in a number of fields including the presence of the ECB at Lord's.' What deceitful nonsense – the MCC Rule 9.2 is simple and cannot be misinterpreted.

    The MCC committee rode roughshod over member rights and privileges at Lord's in October 2015. Their steadfast refusal to publish the ISWP report as a consultative green paper for member action has had a disastrous effect on the process of Royal Charter Incorporation that remains ineffective and incomplete. Four years of hard work and commitment were summarily dismissed.

2. The secretary has failed to adhere to his duty of ensuring the latest sgm process has been followed to the letters of Rule 23.1 (i) to (iv) in sequence. An assistant secretary, on being challenged for starting our sgm at rule 23.1 (iii) has turned the definitive rule process upside down and stated the numbered rule paragraphs are not sequential. Extraordinary.

3. The club regulations list the sovereign *right* of MCC members to attend any general meeting and vote in person. The committee has disenfranchised those members, including myself, who wished to exercise their lawful right to attend our sgm as natural persons. It is for this reason I have refused as a co-signatory to acknowledge an unlawful sgm process being approved by the committee.

B) The SGM Process

1. The secretary is identified in the club rules as the person responsible for the process control itself and has failed to acknowledge the right of the three sgm requisitioners to exercise their freedom to control and record the collection of the necessary 180+ signatures. It was made clear that all signed sgm forms were to be submitted to the membership secretary direct, allowing the censorship of our preamble and the monitoring of the progress of member support. This breach of due process is prejudicial.
2. Club officials had access to the exact voting numbers three days in advance of the actual sgm being convened and our resolution being formally proposed. This led to committee gerrymandering of what should have been a confidential voting process. The following day a report in *The Times* newspaper confirmed a committee initiative to encourage establishment member support in defeating our sgm resolution.
3. This public statement and internal communications circulated by a committee member canvassing support before the sgm had been convened have prejudiced the sgm result.
4. Seeking the support of the president to resolve this dispute (Rule 12A.8) introduces a conflict of interest and a lack of specialist legal knowledge. Our Royal Charter Club deserves better.

C) Conclusion

With one third of the club membership voting, the number can be considered to be a representative sample and therefore can be scaled up to more than 40 per cent of the MCC membership of c18,300 having expressed their wish for change in the autocratic appointment of the new chairman. Siren calls to the committee from c7,500 MCC members will be ignored at your peril.

D) The Solution

To give members the freedom to choose from a NomCo short list of three preferred candidates and select a new club chairman at the 2024 agm. Confirmation of the sole committee appointment at agm using a postal ballot will prove inflammatory and culminate in further member action. QED

Sincerely,
Nigel Knott (Dr.) Elected playing member1966

Carnegie-Brown sent me another very polite reply with nothing of any substance. Guy Lavender, his secretary and chief executive, adopted exactly the same attitude, as did the club solicitor.

And then I wrote to Mark Nicholas, Carnegie-Brown's successor as chairman. Mark, who was president at the time, took over in October 2024. I had given him some confidential documents pertaining to the running of MCC and to my great disappointment he had lost them.

Dear Mark,
1. I learned very early in my life business and friendship are incompatible. Guy Lavender is an employee of MCC and his treatment of me as a very senior member MCC is shameful. Even more so as a fellow veteran commissioned by Queen Elizabeth II, both of whom have a record of decorated service in the army. His behaviour and lack of respect epitomises the unacceptable face of dictatorship and a shocking abuse of power by an MCC employee. I informed him some while ago I objected to being treated by him as another rank under Queen's regulations.
2. Where the lost confidential MCC documents are concerned we will never know of their destination.

However, I wish to make a request for you to obtain another copy of our ISWP final report to the MCC committee dated July 29 2015 and study the contents most carefully. With the support of Oliver Stocken, I was responsible for the ISWP initiative that started the whole overdue process of Incorporation in May 2011. My appointment was conditional.

3. Fortunately, I have kept most of the records of our meetings including a copy of the advice given to Holly Roper Curzon by Farrer & Co that included counsel's opinion on MCC incorporation supplied by Robert Bramwell QC. This opinion is one of the MCC documents that you have lost and Holly will be able to supply another copy as this was a key ingredient to the whole ISWP process of Royal Charter Incorporation which remains uncompleted today. **No sgm has ever been called by MCC committee for member approval of any completed process of Royal Charter incorporation.**

4. If you are to do nothing more in your term of office as MCC chairman but publish and circulate these two documents as green papers for discussion to ALL MCC members, you will have performed an historic act of great significance for the club in my effort to seek the completion of the task of Royal Charter Incorporation without further delay.

5. Our Sovereign King Charles III is our patron and the completion of the Royal Charter Incorporation process an imperative.

Kindest regards,
Nigel.

Nicholas replied:

1 May 2024

Dear Nigel,

I enjoyed meeting you last Thursday, and I greatly respect your dedication to, and knowledge of, the club garnered over the many years of your membership. Having said that, our handshake was in no way an affirmation that I necessarily agree with everything you say. It was – as might be usual among friends after a good lunch – a handshake of genuine warmth and friendship.

I am not yet chair of MCC. I note the points you raise about the 'legality' of the procedures the club follow at the agm, and, if my appointment is confirmed, I will ask our legal team to respond to the points you raise in due course. I personally believe the club conducts its business lawfully and yours is the only dissenting voice I have heard, but I will undertake to establish this beyond all doubt if I find myself at the helm.

Like you, I wish only to see our club run along democratic lines with good governance structures. I have no other agenda, and would certainly wish to dispel any notion of conspiracy within the club.

In respect of your questions about the accounts, I will ask the treasurer to respond to you directly, if answers do not emerge at the agm. Meanwhile, I hope to enjoy today. To be president of MCC at an agm is a formidable challenge but, more importantly, a great honour. I shall give it my best shot and, in doing so, hope collegiate debate and progress make it a worthwhile and enjoyable meeting for all.

As a good friend of mine likes to say – some things you can change, others you can't, and knowing the difference applies to us all!

With good wishes,
Mark

This e-mail was sent 12/11/2024:

Dear Mark,

I hope you are keeping fit and enjoying your new challenges as club chairman.

The recent sgm result over returning some democracy to the club and members' sovereignty being recognised by the committee comes as no surprise as too many members carry serious reservations,

Our central strength until recently has been the defence of our independence as the guardian and trustee of the best interests of our national GAME of cricket and the future of Lord's cricket ground. The two interests are inseparable. All is now threatened by the arrival of mammon at Lord's in the shape of Stanford's ghost. The monetisation of our beloved amateur game has spawned a new version played by mercenaries and MCC seem to be embracing this 'Hundred' behemoth 'London Spirit.'

I am unsurprised by the letter from DCMS as nobody at Lord's has foreseen the dangers in accepting this naked bribe from the ECB and thought about the unintended consequences. Ructions lie ahead. Lord's is a most precious national asset with a huge public support. I mentioned at the 2023 agm the sovereignty of Lord's rests with the freeholders – the MCC members and Charles Rifkind. We are again feeling the effects of the heavy roller being applied by the MCC committee with possible disastrous consequences.

You have chosen to ignore the contents of the important papers I left with you in April this year, I understand they have since been stolen. Amongst them was professional advice from Farrer & Co recommending that Lord's cricket ground should be placed within the secure boundary of a limited liability organisation registered at

Companies House. Our ISWP report embraced this course of action and it has been ignored.

However, the opportunity arises for MCC members to own shares in Lord's plc with a market value on the Stock Exchange of c + £1billion or + £50K for each MCC member at a conservative estimate. This seems to provide a much more attractive solution to our financial situation at Lord's.

I will be publishing a book shortly called *Tunnel Vision at Lord's* and it will chronicle the events of the last 25 years at Lord's. I hope my record of events will put an end to what the Rt Hon Sir Scott Baker described in 2002 as a "self-perpetuating oligarchy." I will be funding the cost of a free copy for the 18,000 MCC members from my estate for them to read the inside story of MCC.

Kindest regards
Sincerely,
Nigel

I received no response. I was to learn subsequently that Nicholas had left my documents in a briefcase, which apparently was stolen. They were not recovered.

In conclusion, I would submit that Lord Hugh Griffiths MC PC and Ted Dexter were the two outstanding presidents during my time, with Colin Cowdrey and Stephen Fry the two worst. Charles Fry, who was the chairman to support my personal view that proxy voting should be introduced at agm's, as he thought this a good idea, was the best of the chairmen and Gerald Corbett the worst since inauguration in 2000. I would say Keith Bradshaw was the best secretary/ceo and Roger Knight the worst.

And now we arrive at the central conundrum: Why waste time and energy supporting an out of date management structure past its sell by date and not move with the times?

Cricket played at Lord's is being monetised by the arrival of The Hundred, so why not monetise Lord's itself and reward the owners – the MCC members – by enabling them to exercise their sovereignty and ownership of Lord's through becoming shareholders, at a special general meeting?

Keith Bradshaw (left) Charles Rifkind (centre) and Derek Brewer Reminiscing over the life at being a secretary and chief executive at MCC

How Lord's looked in 1999

Chapter 11
A New Landlord at Lord's
Documenting the changes needed

Lot 11

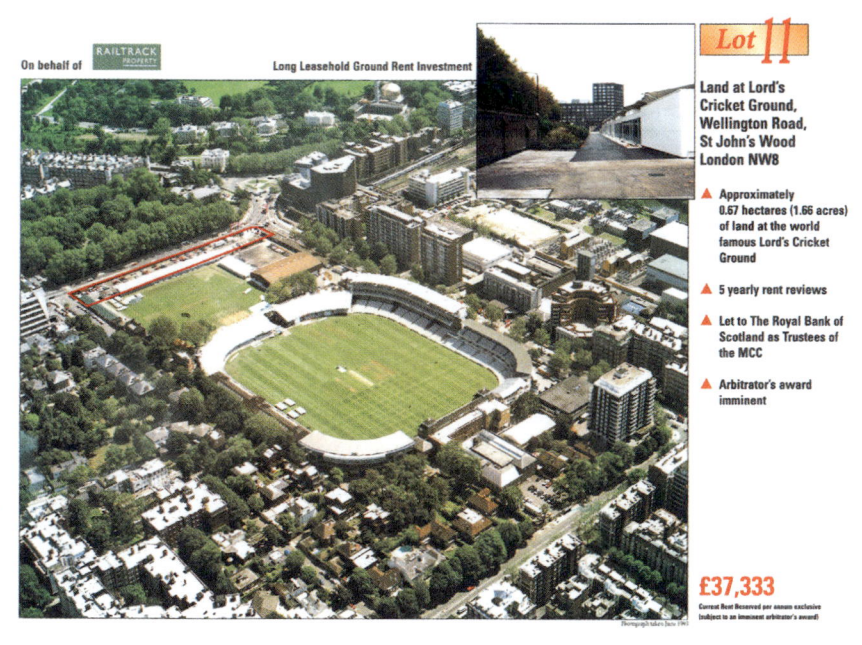

The details of Lot 11 from the auction in 1999

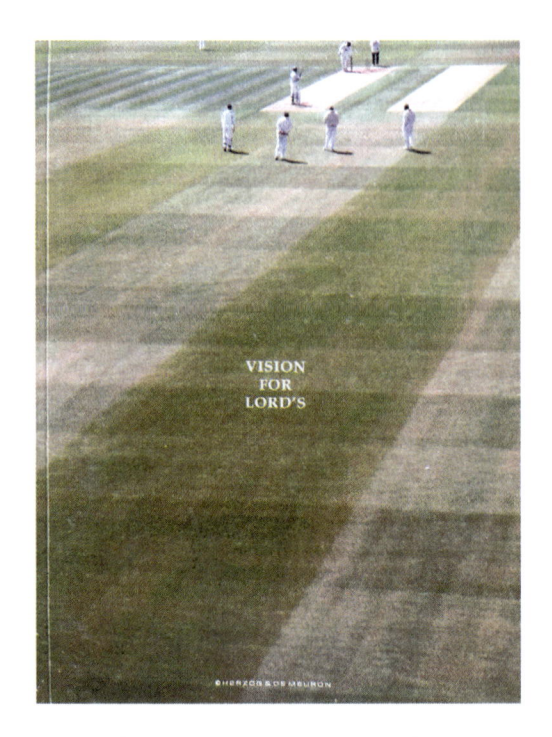

Vision for Lord's Cover – Herzog & de Meuron

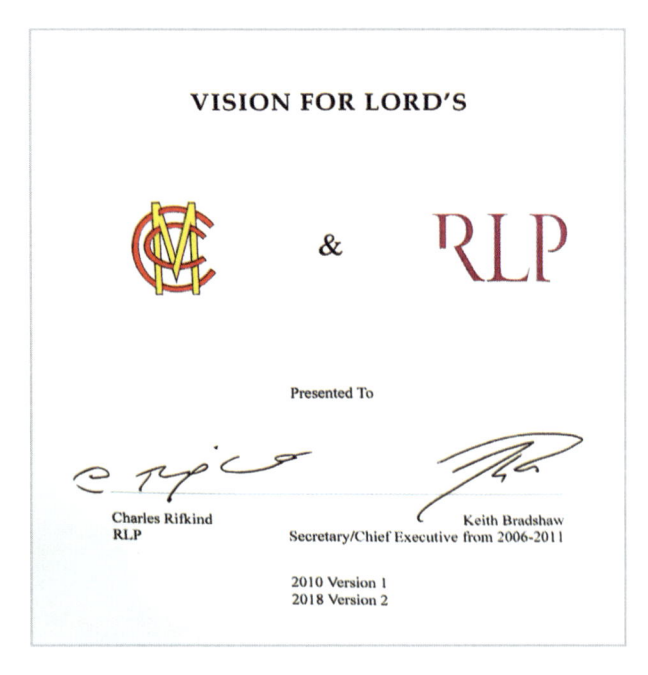

Vision for Lord's – Signature page

As we approach the 10th Anniversary of the first publication of this document we should reflect that whilst the passage of time has not yet yielded this development, it has afforded us the perspective of a lost opportunity.

If a different decision had been made in 2008, and the scheme, which had been unanimously supported by the MCC development committee then including Sir John Major, had been allowed to proceed, then Lord's in 2018 would deservedly be sitting amongst the world's best-in-class sporting venues, would have significant financial resources and would have perhaps removed itself from the burden of a rental liability.

We would ask you as reader to be tolerant of the exact design of the Herzog & de Meuron scheme. To some extent it was merely to inform and masterplan the potential opportunity. Without question, what is clear is that emphasis will be placed on the delivery of high quality architecture and design. Lord's, the location and its international significance demands it.

Let us remember the boldness of vision from previous committees which led to the commissioning of the Media Centre, and its construction by boat builders in Cornwall. At some point in the future we hope that the Committee will embrace the same confidence of purpose to profitably reshape the future of their club.

As we go to publication in 2018, we note that fees of the membership are set to rise well above inflation.

Within this booklet lies the genesis of an alternative strategy designed to return members benefits, reduce the long-term liabilities of the club and finally show some return for the MCC's £10m million investment into both this scheme and the other presented stalled scheme on the South West corner.

Future generations will decide when, and if, such a grand scheme can be delivered, but the red line is clear: the game must continue to be played, celebrated and cherished at Lord's.

Today we also witness the launch of New Commonwealth, an initiative which liberates the conventions of property investment and opens up ownership to everyone. For Lord's specifically, it enables cricket-lovers from around the world to participate in their passion – and own a piece of this famous ground. Let us hope that the expected groundswell of opinion that accompanies the launch of this new "common wealth" will inspire the guardians of this great club to act, rather than witness another fallow and frustrating decade.

The new owners, perhaps thousands of you, will be informed of the ongoing deliberations, invited to attend events and given a platform for your opinion. And, in the future when the MCC lease expires, or before, your descendants will inherit the share of the unencumbered land.

But those participating in the purchase of land at The Nursery End at Lord's should not be under any illusion: the long-term development rights are possible but negotiation with the MCC is challenging, and might well prove fruitless.

In purchasing a piece of the Nursery ground at Lord's, perhaps as a token of your appreciation for this great game, a gift for the grandchildren or simply as a souvenir of happy days spectating, you are also making a modest bet. One day we might see this ground redeveloped, and then you will be financially rewarded. But whilst the odds are long, the ownership remains in perpetuity.

For more information about subscribing to our offer visit newcommonwealth.com

Keith Bradshaw
Secretary/Chief Executive
(2006-2011)

Vision for Lord's

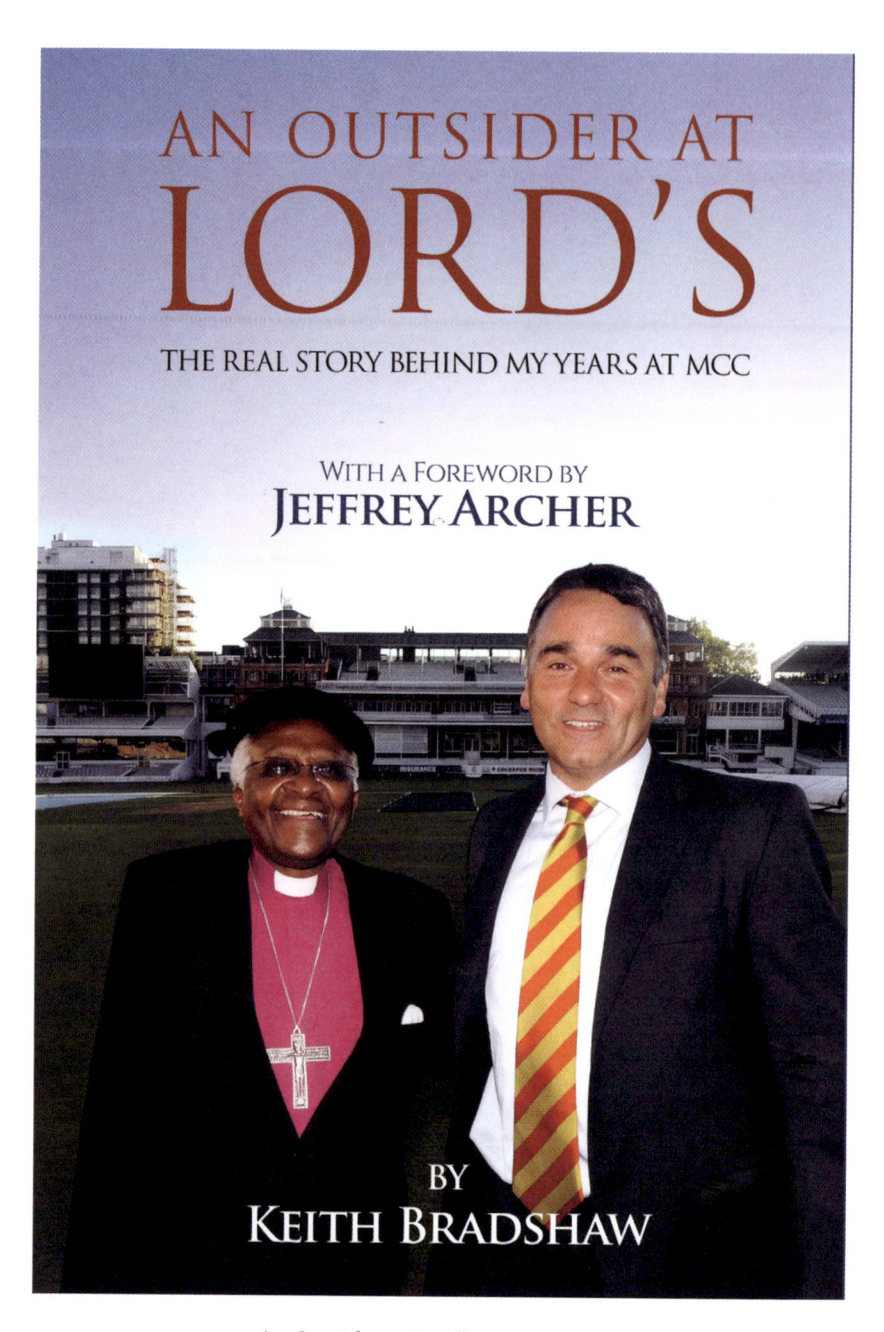

An Outsider at Lord's – Front Cover

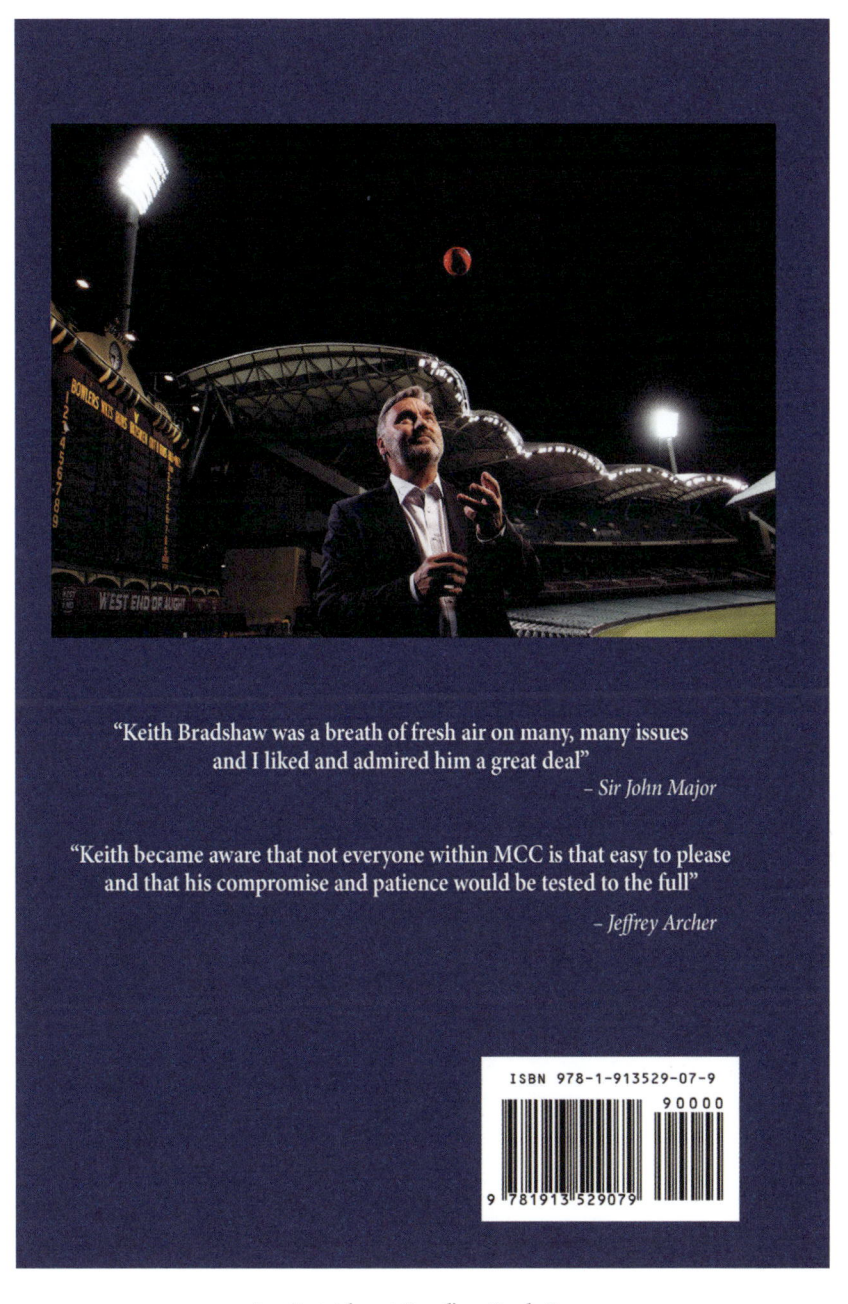

"Keith Bradshaw was a breath of fresh air on many, many issues and I liked and admired him a great deal"

– Sir John Major

"Keith became aware that not everyone within MCC is that easy to please and that his compromise and patience would be tested to the full"

– Jeffrey Archer

ISBN 978-1-913529-07-9

An Outsider at Lord's – Back Cover

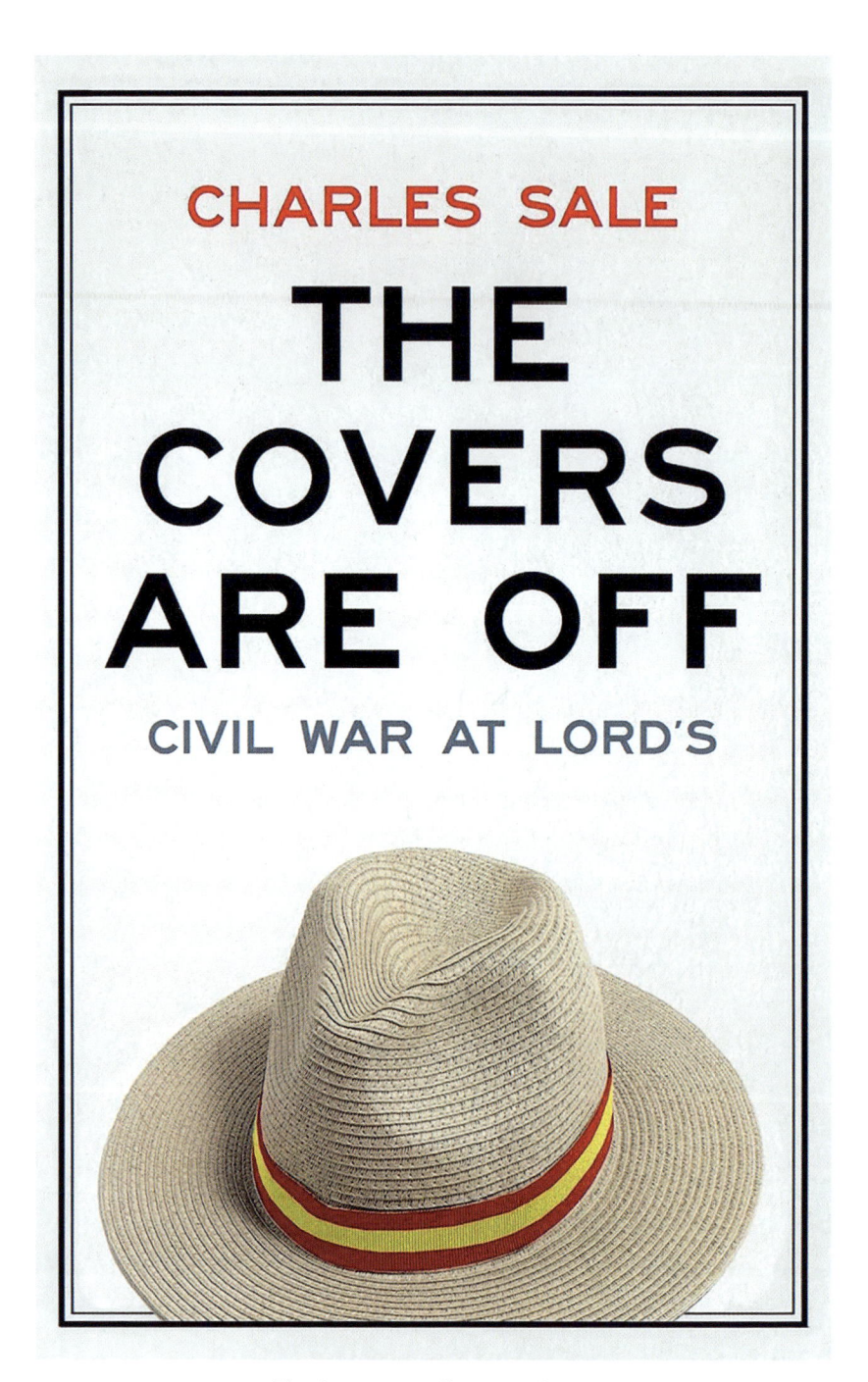

The Covers are off – Front Cover
Reproduced by kind permission of Charles Sale

The last two decades have seen a civil war inside MCC over the future of Lord's, though the club's membership have largely been kept in the dark. On the one side, the MCC establishment; on the other, the property developer Charles Rifkind, who bought the rights to develop the railway tunnels under the ground's Nursery End from under the noses of MCC.

Rifkind's audacious purchase led to two decades of frustration, as MCC rebuffed his attempts to bring the 'Home of Cricket' into the twenty-first century. It is a saga that saw the cricketing establishment take sides in an increasingly acrimonious conflict, which played out in furious debates behind the closed Grace Gates.

With a cast list that includes a former prime minister, several England Test captains, leaders of finance and industry and committed agitators amongst the MCC membership, *The Covers Are Off* reveals a bitter struggle between the guardians of tradition and a new order intent on change.

ISBN 978-1-912914-30-2

The Covers are off – Back Cover

"Why is the cat looking so happy?"

Chapter 12 – Conclusion
A golden opportunity awaits – a property owning democracy at Lord's

Chapter 12
Conclusion

During my time as an MCC member the character of the club and the culture at Lord's has changed dramatically: from 1966, the year I was elected, when England teams were synonymous with MCC, to today, when the club displays the decadent signs of a loss of identity and power. The proportion of elected playing members to ordinary members has been considerably reduced from close to 100 per cent in 1867 to fewer than ten per cent today. This despite the fact MCC had acquired its prestige from fielding world-class XIs and being the owner of the finest and most valuable ground in the world.

The winds of change began in 1968 when politics decreed that a private member club was not deemed acceptable to govern the game and receive public funds. It happened at a challenging time for MCC at the height of the political row centred on the Basil d'Oliveira affair and the cancellation of tours to and from South Africa. The controversy over Afghanistan in 2025 was a further example of the use of Lord's without members' consent.

This period since has been accompanied by far too many disputes at Lord's. The club is now a significant business without the necessary executive structure and business management skills in place to guarantee future success and profitability.

The government of MCC in 1866 consisted of a committee of eight officers and 16 elected representatives. Today, the government of the committee is accompanied by an explosion in unelected sub-committee members, all of whom have quasi executive powers, accompanied by a reduction in the numbers and powers of elected representatives to a small minority. Most significant has been the removal of the traditional powers and responsibilities of the trustees themselves. The committee has assumed unbridled executive powers in the absence of any checks and balances (company secretary) or court of appeal (trustees).

The Incorporation and Structure Working Party (ISWP) report contained proposals designed to address unacceptable management failures. The central theme of the report remains the restoration of the influence and powers of elected representatives forming a members' committee and the creation of an executive team with delegated powers endowed by the main committee to a board of directors to manage Lord's as a wholly owned limited company. The trustee duties and responsibilities must be reinstated.

Sir Michael Jenkins, self-appointed as the first chairman of MCC, would look at a committee colleague in disbelief if no opinion was expressed upon a matter affecting the future of the club. He was known to reply: "I see." That meant in reality no further promotion within the club hierarchy. A withering stare of death!

This whole unhappy saga and the behaviour of the committee brings to mind Macaulay's words "Large promises, smooth excuses, elaborate tissues of circumstantial falsehood, chicanery, perjury and forgery are the weapons offensive and defensive of …" All of the vile ingredients that make any gentleman's agreement impossible. I can add my own personal experience. My conversation with a trustee (Robert Leigh) and the deputy secretary (Colin Maynard) informed me, while I was serving on the ISWP, that any future development at Lord's would be piecemeal and financed by the MCC membership alone. They made it crystal clear to me that under no circumstances should Charles Rifkind gain any benefit from any future ground development at Lord's.

It is only with hindsight I can recognise the mysterious intervention of Maynard at our ISWP meeting held on March 2 2015. I am recorded in the meeting minutes as accusing him of "throwing sand in our eyes" by causing division and confusion. The chairman designate, Gerald Corbett, who had been invited as a matter of courtesy to the meeting, wasted no time in supporting Colin and expressing an objection to an elected members committee proposal before being ordered by the WP chairman Peter Leaver QC to "shut up!"

After our final report was submitted to the committee on July 29 2015 the then president (David Morgan) announced our dissolution in a letter to members dated August 20 2015. Corbett announced in an MCC newsletter: "There is no appetite for change" despite the ISWP having spent two and a half years producing the necessary restructuring details for the committee to establish MCC as a Royal Charter Corporation. I can therefore share the emotional reactions expressed by Robert Griffiths and his 'Vision' development committee on suffering a similar fate.

The president's letter effectively guillotined the whole ISWP restructuring process despite the fact the committee had actively supported our efforts since the grant of the Royal Charter in 2012. Very significant club funds had been expended, including specialist professional advice. This time I appealed to the trustees (messrs Anthony Wreford, Derek Underwood and Andrew Beeson) to warn the committee it was committed to implement the binding obligations given to the membership in connection with the ISWP final report. There was no reply.

My own reaction was even more emphatic as Oliver Stocken, Corbett's predecessor, had assured me over lunch at the Garrick Club in March 2011 that ISWP could decide our own agenda and our final recommendations following incorporation were to be made the subject of a consultative green paper to be submitted to the membership without any committee interference. Subsequent events do not cover Stocken in glory given he was at the centre of the 'Vision' dispute. The troubling ingredient is the complete failure of the membership to prevent the committee riding roughshod over the efforts of those who have given their time and resources freely, acting, the membership believes, in the best interests of MCC.

Successive club chairmen have acted *ultra vires* with the assumption of executive powers that are not endowed in them by the club rules. Perhaps worst of all is the conflict of opinion expressed by Stocken and Corbett, whose committees commissioned the ISWP in the first instance.

*

Covid struck not only the health of the nation but also the economic health and management of MCC. Unlike some sporting bodies like Wimbledon, the Jockey Club and many cricket clubs, MCC failed to have any business interruption insurance policy in place, leaving a big hole in the finances which required emergency financing through the sale of life memberships. A further issue was that such individuals jumped the long waiting list.

An unexpected side effect of the statutory legislation preventing MCC member meetings taking place at Lord's has resulted in the temporary measures being embedded permanently in the club rules. The electronic virtual world arrived with no express permission within the rules for virtual (online) meetings to address this crisis. Physical attendance of members at any general meeting was not allowed under the health protection (Coronavirus restrictions) regulations applicable in England.

The committee did not believe that the restrictions would be relaxed sufficiently to enable a physical sgm meeting to be held in October 2020. To ensure that the club fully complied with the law, the committee had to make emergency amendments (described as 'temporary') to the rules specifically to allow general meetings to take place in a manner which was not repugnant or contrary to the law or inconsistent with the provisions of the club's Royal Charter. In other words, by way of a virtual meeting with online voting deployed besides postal voting, so as to encourage participation by members. These temporary measures were designed to facilitate decision-making and not to disenfranchise members from exercising their fundamental right of voting on business to be put forward at a general meeting.

The situation has transpired to be the thin end of a very large wedge with the committee recognising the attractive cost savings delivered by virtual meetings held online. What was initially an emergency measure has since been normalised. A 'virtual' sgm was held in March 2024 despite the fact that the club regulations define attending and voting at general meetings being member 'rights!'

This novel digitised world has developed into a lawyer playground with words being used and defined in the manner of *Alice in Wonderland*. In correspondence with the Privy Council office the words 'natural persons' have appeared, presumably to describe MCC members being part of a chartered corporation, seemingly to differentiate them from being virtual persons!

Rule 25.4 voting – 'A resolution put to the vote of the meeting shall be decided on a show of hands unless the MCC committee has decided prior to the agm that the resolution is subject to postal voting or electronic voting or both.' So how do the natural persons attending the meeting vote, if the committee decides voting should be other than by a show of hands? In the early days of my membership, the club's agm was pure theatre with speakers using their gifted powers of oratory to enjoy controlling an audience willing to indict an overpowering president. Whilst MCC members looked forward to a special occasion, the MCC committee did not.

Perhaps the most important items to be transacted at any agm fall within the 'ordinary business agenda' that has now been proscribed with an explanatory note on all agm documentation. 'The MCC committee considers that all items of business on the agenda of the agm which require a vote are of sufficient importance to the club to justify the use of electronic and postal voting to enable all full and senior members to vote without having to be present at the time of the meeting.' Proxy voting has been expunged from the club rules.

Contrast this with the old Rule 21 'All business shall be deemed special that is transacted at a special general meeting and also all business that is transacted at an annual general meeting with the **exception** of any ordinary business.'

Ordinary business used to include the appointment or re-appointment of club trustees, club chairman, chairman of finance, club auditors, newly elected committee members, and the adoption of the report and accounts. Each of these items required a simple majority for approval.

*

This is the detail of an e-mail sent by me, dated November 22 2018 to Guy Lavender (secretary) and Adam Chadwick (museum curator):

> Dear Guy/Adam,
>
> Thank you for the time you spent with Alan Meyer and myself at Lord's on November 19.
>
> It was good to see you both again - our meeting to discuss the specific matter of the MCC trustees was of some significance. As you both recognise, I have spent countless hours researching the history of the Lord's trust and the paper I produced on February 2 2011 for the constitution WP, which was chaired by Keith Bradshaw, provides important background evidence. Whilst the veracity of this evidence is reliable and well documented, the three proposals I made at the time remain unaddressed after more than seven years. I can only hope you will help to resolve things to the satisfaction of all concerned.
>
> Following our discussions I wish to emphasise the fact that the ISWP raised two issues of significance relating

to the trustees in our report to the committee dated July 29 2015:

Para 13: 'It might be thought sensible to have Lord's held in trust so that nobody could execute against the club's ground.'

Para 73: 'The trustees…will have full trustee act duties and responsibilities.'

The grant of the Royal Charter enabled the ISWP to review the structure of the club and most importantly to recommend long overdue change. In truth there is no need to make any revolutionary changes to resolve the trust concerns, as my detailed review of the history of the MCC trustees reveals that a breach of trust has taken place with the committee failing to accept the fact that a Lord's trust was originally created in 1866 and the trustees were endowed with trustee act powers (ref trustee deed of conveyance August 31 1937). By returning to the status quo ante the necessary protection of Lord's cricket ground will be restored and the trustees will have their trustee act powers reinstated. Article 14 of the Royal Charter needs to be amended accordingly together with the club rules. No other action will be required.

I wish to provide further important historical detail to the paper I circulated dated February 2 2011:

1. The status, duties and responsibilities of the MCC trustees were expressly stated originally in the club rules of 1867 at VII (a), IX, X and XII
    a) Rules XII (b) and XIII of 1946 confirmed the trustees as ex-officio members of the committee enjoying statutory powers
    b) The number of trustees was reduced to four in 1951
    c) Following Sir Pelham Warner's retirement from office owing to ill health in the number of

trustees was reduced to the minimum number of three, 1962

d) In 1964 the committee removed the trustee lifetime terms of office together with their duty to appoint their successors. For this reason I have requested sight of the nine trustee death certificates as these may prove that the 6th Earl of Dartmouth, who died in 1936, was replaced by his son and he, Baron Hawke, Sir Francis Lacey, Sir Francis Jackson and Josiah Webbe were the last lifetime appointments. If the nine death certificates are all contiguous, it suggests the trustee legal instruments were all held within the club archives.

It is possible therefore the deed of trust ordered by the committee in 1866 was considered to be implicit within the context of the five deeds of appointment relating to the original five trustees, with Lord's being conveyed into their ownership 'for the benefit of the club' in perpetuity.

Therefore termination of lifetime officeholder trustees accompanied by their power of appointing replacements ordered by the committee in 1964 was in breach of the trustee act of 1906.

2. A new trustee (Earl of Dartmouth) took office via a deed of appointment dated August 30 1937 and a deed of conveyance was signed by the trustees the following day to appoint a custodian trustee (Glyn Mills).

Response from Guy Lavender:

Dear Nigel and Alan,

I'm most grateful to you both for meeting me on November 19 to discuss the specific matter of a trust deed and, more broadly, the role of the club's trustees. I found it helpful to listen to your views in this regard and I do understand why these matters are important to you. I also undertook to reply directly as the club's chief executive and you should be assured that I do that with independence and in good faith.

Having considered the matter carefully, I remain of the view that there is no imperative to instruct lawyers to go to the High Court for a legal determination or to take further legal advice with regard to the existence or otherwise of a trust deed or the roles and responsibilities of the trustees. That judgment is based on a lack of evidence of the existence of a trust deed combined with legal advice the club has previously taken and which indicates there is no requirement to investigate the matter further. Moreover, that view is also held by the Privy Council, with whom we have had the opportunity to liaise in connection with the club's Royal Charter. This, together with the club's rules, clearly articulates the governance arrangements of the club. In turn, it is not sensible for the club to expend additional resources or time investigating these matters.

From my perspective, the governance of the club continues to evolve and I do think it would be useful to review the relevant powers and responsibilities of those charged with running this unique and special club moving forward. By definition, that would also include the role of the trustees and it is a matter I will address during the course of next year.

Yours sincerely, Guy Lavender, secretary ceo MCC

From Adam Chadwick, curator MCC:

Nigel

Thanks for your e-mail and your patience with regard to the time it has taken me to reply. While it may be a surprise to you and others, definitive papers do not exist on such matters.

It is clear that the issues around the trustees and ownership of property have been central to much of the club's discussions over the past few years and I know you have been much involved, most recently with the ISWP. I believe this work has contributed significantly to a far more accurate picture of the club's past but I am not party to decision making on the club's future path and so cannot comment on that with any accuracy.

Please see our specific comments below on the factual detail of your document:

Under the heading 'Confirmation of Trust – The Evidence' you state that death certificates and the deed of appointment are held in the club archives. They are not held here; they are held with the deeds off site (Dechert LLP London), which I have not seen. I would recommend that you distinguish what is held here and what is held off site.

Under the heading 'The Lord's Trust,' you state that the decision to purchase the freehold was undertaken at the special general meeting on May 3 1865. There is no mention of this in the minutes. You are right about the fact that proposals to place the property in the hands of the trustees was approved at the same meeting, but the decision to purchase the freehold, and create a donations fund provisionally for that purpose, was initially suggested at a meeting of the committee on April 8 1864; the decision was then definitively made on March 26 1866 when the committee resolved to use Nicholson's money to purchase the freehold from Isaac Moses Marsden.

You state that the five trustees were appointed for life at the annual meeting of April 8 1864. This is incorrect; they were not appointed until the committee meeting on May 23 1864.

I hope this is helpful.

Yours sincerely
Adam

From me to Holly Roper-Curzon
MCC assistant secretary (legal):
November 25 2019

Dear Holly,

Thank you for your e-mail of November 18 2019.

The rule of law depends upon certainty and the administration of natural justice. How I wish that you as MCC"s chief law officer together with your professional colleagues would adopt the lessons of Hamlet and apply pure reason to the matters relating to the club trustees and the history of MCC. Where any scintilla of doubt exists, you should rely on the historical evidence to establish the truth. Think it is just possible you may be mistaken in adopting your position as a Lord's trust denier.

To allow the secretary at Lord's to guillotine my efforts to determine the truth in matters with a troubled conscience: like a computer, if you feed defective instructions to the lawyers you consult, flawed opinions are bound to follow as is presently the case.

I now refer to your latest communication and thank you for the clarification concerning the dissolution of the MCC Royal Charter article 14 being sovereign. In the light of the evidence I have provided from the club archives, the MCC members cannot be entitled to benefit from proprietary rights described in rule 26 and enjoy a windfall financial gain. This in bald terms could be the result of rule 26 being determined.

It is with great respect I have to bring to your notice as the MCC law officer that you, your professional advisors and some of your committee colleagues cannot continue in a state of denial on the subject of the Lord's trust and its history. Please find attached a copy of my 'memorandum of evidence' dated February 2 2011 that was presented to the MCC ceo Keith Bradshaw at the time and later to the Incorporation and Structure WP for action.

In addition I wish to make a formal complaint (rule 6) concerning Guy Lavender's decision to guillotine any further correspondence with me on these important matters:

"Whilst I would not wish to attempt to restrict any member in his or her quest to receive information regarding the club, it is, at the same time, my responsibility to ensure that the time of the secretariat and staff is spent in such a manner as to provide to all members with a proper and efficient service. There must come a point, therefore, at which it is detrimental for the club in general to devote large amounts of time to correspondence received from one member in particular."

This represents a naked abuse of power. His actions do not accord with reason and fairness, nor do his actions seem to have been authorised in accordance with Rule 6 (i) or (ii). I have been deprived of basic rights and privileges to which as a long-standing member of MCC I am entitled to enjoy. His unacceptable sanctions are more in keeping with those of a military junta than MCC.

When I consider the time and money I have spent serving my club over very many years and representing MCC on the field of play, this is rather shabby. treatment. My recent correspondence drawing the secretary's attention to the fact the MCC website home page contains material errors and the Lord's website home page is defective in the history of Lord's has been ignored. My attempts to chronicle and record accurately a vital part of MCC history are being wilfully obstructed.

The memorandum (see attached) provided by the past club solicitor, Alan Meyer, dated January 22 includes an early example of a possible breach of trust identified at the seventh para. This memorandum contains some unrecorded history relating to the events that culminated in the rejection of the bicentenary report and accounts in 1987.

In law the word 'trustee' has a very specific meaning, tracing back to when it was first used by the MCC committee in 1864 with the creation of five trustees. The word has been in existence ever since and Sir Scott Baker in his Structure WP report (2002) expressed his confusion over the role of the trustees.

Please submit this correspondence, accompanied by the two attached files, to every member of the MCC committee soonest, with a request for a formal investigation into the matter of the MCC trustees and the MCC committee orders made on March 26 1866 for 'The five trustees to execute a deed of trust' and on August 22 1866 for 'Lord's ground to be vested in the trustees' being entrenched in MCC Rule XII of 1867.

Sincerely
Nigel

*

The London Spirit franchise, seemingly a beguiling bribe to guarantee the ECB's future access to Lord's and further undermine MCC's independence comes at a time of financial concern. It sems to me the top priority of the club's hierarchy is to complete the incorporation process begun in December 2012 and install a top-class board of directors to manage Lord's plc as a successful commercial enterprise.

The days of MCC volunteers tinkering with executive management decisions must end. The evidence of this failed business model is there for all to see with the present management model being out of touch and out of date. Nothing but root and branch restructuring will bring about the necessary future prosperity at Lord's.

The opportunity is staring MCC members in the face – a six-acre world-class cricket arena with another 11 acres of land awaiting holistic development to generate spectacular capital and income gains for MCC. Just imagine the many wasted £millions spent on the 'Vision for Lord's' being recovered and put to good use in a new holistic 'Super Vision for Lord's' to include world-class branded facilities for indoor sports such as darts, snooker and bowls, to name but a few. Lord's would set a new trend in excellence with brand new Tavern and Allen stands. Not to mention a prestigious hotel for members and players' use and high quality residential/commercial accommodation. No longer will the ECB determine Test match ground standards – MCC will lead by example at Lord's.

The basis of a future commercial enterprise is in place at Lord's with a chartered corporation shell structure providing the mechanism to facilitate the necessary structural changes in the management of Lord's. MCC members have to make a game-changing decision at a difficult time. It is no longer a question of slavishly paying annual subscriptions by standing order and appearing every year at Lord's to watch a Test match. It is completing the process that began in December 2012 and awaits delivery: 'The members of the said unincorporated association (MCC) and all such persons as may hereafter become members of the one body corporate hereby constituted shall forever hereafter be one body corporate by the name of 'Marylebone Cricket Club.'

It is abundantly clear 'one corporate body' does not yet exist. Period. And so why since 2012 have three consecutive MCC chairmen failed to seek committee approval to complete the process in accordance with Royal Charter article 1 above? The seventh chairman in office today has shown no signs of changing the status quo. Perhaps of more relevance is a glaring absence of any democratic accountability. The formation of one body corporate known as MCC will terminate the arcane management structure in place at Lord's since 1866.

A new dawn awaits: MCC members endowed with the necessary sovereignty to conserve the future of the traditional game of red ball cricket at the world headquarters in perpetuity. The world of cricket is undergoing rapid change and the present management structure of MCC is ill-equipped to address the threats to the club and its valuable property interests. It is urgent therefore to complete the constitution of one body corporate at Lord's as required by Royal Charter article 1. This completion process will enable MCC members to become an integral part of the one body corporate bringing significant new shareholder benefits. The completion of a 'tunnel vision' application form is a vital first step to enable MCC members to transition from a subscription to a shareholding model offered by the one MCC body corporate. QED.

This could be YOURS!
Go to www.mccsgm.org.uk to sign up
Password – Ward2025

More MCC history @ www.mccmembers.co.uk

"...and play stopped due to movement behind the bowler's arm..."

Postscript

On 12 December 2012 HRH Queen Elizabeth II granted 18,000 MCC Members an instrument of democratic change – Her Royal Charter. Since that historic date a few unelected Committee bigots have resisted the necessary restructuring at Lord's. Two organisations exist today domiciled at Lords Ground A) the traditional unincorporated members club to which members continue to pay annual subscriptions and B) a dormant shell company No. RC 000862 registered at Companies House. Lord's Cricket Ground itself is registered as BB 6624 in the ownership of Marylebone Cricket Club.

The management of Royal Charter Company No 000862 is a complete mystery regulated by an arcane committee structure, swollen with its own authority, riding roughshod over the rights and liberties of MCC Members. The underlying doctrine of the long existent feudal custom of the sovereignty of the rule of law has been misunderstood and buried at Lord's, with the principles of the Magna Carta of 1215 long forgotten and denied to MCC members.

Thirteen years is far too long for MCC Members to have tolerated what has become an uncertain Royal Charter interregnum. It is time to hear the hoarse voice of Member tumult at Lord's on May Day 2025 in demanding the necessary democratic changes at Lord's and to enjoy the "Presents" that flow from Queen Elizabeth II's Royal Charter.

The Elephant in the Committee Room
Equality, Diversity and Inclusivity (EDI) are championed by the MCC Committee and yet obvious Discrimination exists

within an undemocratic and unjust Post Code Lottery membership structure denying the basic entitlement to a reserved seat in return for a membership subscription of many £00's. Those members domiciled between 40–100 miles from Central London are considered to enjoy an urban existence. Try telling this group of members that living in SN12 has an equal chance of obtaining a seat at a Test Match as those living in NW8.

The Wellington Road/St John's Wood Road Big Match Queues at Lord's are an egregious example of an MCC Subscription Swindle.

Determining the constitution of one Royal Charter Body Corporate at Lord's will bring a basic Shareholder entitlement of owning a member seat at all events staged at Lord's Cricket Ground.

Introducing Shareholder property rights at Lord's with Freeholder Member Seats will remove any ECB power to deny MCC Members free access to Lord's as a lawful right.

10th March 2025

Index

A
Aberfan disaster 35
Aldershot 37
Alexander, Lord 162, 165–166, 175
Allen, Gubby 11, 54, 93, 185
Almacantar 134, 136–137, 139–141
Army 29, 31, 37–38

B
Bailey, Jack 23, 67–69, 77, 81–82, 90, 117, 165
Baker, Sir Scott 16, 18, 50–51, 120, 149, 152, 166, 196, 219
Batts, David 141
Belfast 36–38
Bradshaw, Keith 20, 22, 99, 117–118, 120–122, 134, 140, 144, 166, 176, 179, 196, 212, 218
Brewer, Derek 118, 134, 179

C
Carnegie-Brown, Bruce 161, 185–186, 188, 192
Clark, David 67, 69, 81–82, 90
Compton, Denis 32
Corbett, Gerald 49, 161, 165–167, 179, 182, 184–185, 196, 209–210
Cowdrey, Lord 23, 56, 69–70, 77–78, 82, 145, 196

D
Dental Practice 38
Doggart, Hubert 83, 90
Dowley, Justin 17, 118, 122, 135–136, 141–142, 164, 166

E
England and Wales Cricket Board 8, 100, 104–105
Entry Fees for World Cup 47

F
Fitzgerald, R A 9, 11
Friction with ECB 45
Fry, Charles 22, 61, 66, 94, 112–113, 118, 162–163, 166, 176, 196
Fry, Sir Stephen 40, 196

G
Gandon, Nick 134
George Mann 16, 61, 68, 72
Grabiner, Lord 120, 129, 133–135, 138–139
Griffiths, Lord 20, 23, 46, 52–57, 60, 96, 196
Robert Griffiths 113–114, 120, 142–143, 167–169, 209
Guy's Hospital 21, 31, 34

Index

H
Highgate School 32, 34
Hobbs, Jack 6
Hodson, Philip 25, 112, 129, 163
Holmes, Percy 6, 142

I
Insole, Doug 68, 85–86

J
Jenkins, Sir Michael 48, 61–62, 112, 116, 131, 161–163, 165–167, 170, 208

K
Knight, Roger 112, 116–117, 140, 163, 168, 173–174, 196
Knott, James 29
Knott, Nigel 1–3, 53–54, 57–59, 90–91, 96–97, 100, 102, 106, 114, 142, 167, 172–173, 175, 182–183, 187, 189, 192
Knott, Rosemary 31–32, 34
Knott, Sydney 29
Knott, William 29

L
Lavender, Guy 14–15, 97, 145, 149, 192, 214–215, 218
Leaver, Peter 23, 179, 183, 209
Lewis, Tony 47, 57, 61, 82, 112–116, 120, 168
London Spirit 7–8, 12, 195, 219
Lord's plc 196, 219
Lord, Thomas 5

M
Major matches at Lord's 72
Major, Sir John 57, 118, 120, 123, 129–130, 137, 142
Maynard, Colin 167, 208–209
MCC agm and rejection of accounts 22–23, 40, 46, 56, 68–69, 73, 76, 158, 219
MCC chairmen and presidents 161
MCC committee mismanagement 15
MCC loss of status 21
MCC sgm 81, 189
MCC trustees 16, 144, 149–153, 155–159, 212–213, 219
McGowan, Brian 139
McInerny, Clare Henriette 29
Melluish, Michael 24–25, 53, 60–61
Meyer, Alan 54, 57–59, 68, 71–72, 85, 87, 171, 212
Moses, Isaac 6, 9, 112, 216

N
Nicholas, Mark 162, 165, 192–193, 196
Nicholson, William 6–7, 16, 155–156, 216

P
Penang 36
Peters, Nigel 59

R
Railtrack 12, 19, 111–115, 124, 127, 136, 140, 164, 179, 185
Reason, John 40
Rice, Sir Tim 24
Rifkind, Charles 19, 24, 26, 63, 111–112, 116, 118, 120–121, 124–125, 136, 140–141, 147, 167, 176, 184–185, 195, 197, 208
Robertson, Sir Simon 134, 138
Roper-Curzon, Holly 186, 217
Royal Charter 10, 14–16, 22–23, 31–32, 45, 49–50, 65–66, 96, 98, 100, 128, 144, 149, 152–154, 182, 187, 189–191, 193, 209–210, 213, 215, 217, 220–221
Russell, Lord 6, 9–11, 95, 97, 159

S
Sale, Charles 19
Silk, Dennis 13, 16, 46–47, 95, 102, 170
Stanford, Allen 21–22, 195
Stocken, Oliver 17, 23, 112, 118, 122, 135, 137–138, 141–142, 161, 163–167, 179, 184, 193, 209–210
Subba Row, Raman 16, 23, 70

T
Test and County Cricket Board 8, 16, 20, 72
The Hundred 7, 93, 197
Trueman, Freddie 32
Trustees 149, 151, 155

V
Vision for Lord's 10, 17, 23, 122, 129–131, 134, 143, 153, 166, 184, 220

W
Ward, William 5–6, 13
Woodcock, John 68–70, 152
Wreford, Anthony 112, 163, 209

You can become a Shareholder of Lord's Plc

- *Lord's Ground Match Seat for Life*

- *No more queuing*

- *Shareholding in Lord's Plc*

- *Share transferable for value*

- *Dividend income*

- *Introduction of Company Law*

- *Termination of arbitrary committee government*

- *A world class Body Corporate – the MCC*

* Go to <u>www.mccsgm.org.uk</u> to bring about change at Lord's *

Password – Ward2025

You can become a Shareholder of Lord's Plc

- *Lord's Ground Match Seat for Life*

- *No more queuing*

- *Shareholding in Lord's Plc*

- *Share transferable for value*

- *Dividend income*

- *Introduction of Company Law*

- *Termination of arbitrary committee government*

- *A world class Body Corporate – the MCC*

* Go to www.mccsgm.org.uk to bring about change at Lord's *

Password – Ward2025

"He finally managed to go underground."